P9-DDM-663

Finding God

Where You Least Expect Him

John
FISCHER

WITHDRAWN

HARVEST HOUSE™ PUBLISHERS

EUGENE, OREGON

Unless otherwise indicated, Scripture quotations are taken from the Holy Bible, Today's New International Version™ Copyright © 2001 by International Bible Society. All rights reserved.

Verses marked NIV are taken from the Holy Bible: New International Version®. NIV®. Copyright © 1973, 1978, 1984 by the International Bible Society. Used by permission of Zondervan Publishing House. The "NIV" and "New International Version" trademarks are registered in the United States Patent and Trademark Office by International Bible Society.

Verses marked NASB are taken from the New American Standard Bible®, © 1960, 1962, 1963, 1968, 1971, 1972, 1973, 1975, 1977, 1995 by The Lockman Foundation. Used by permission.

Verses marked KJV are taken from the King James Version of the Bible.

Cover by Left Coast Design, Portland, Oregon

Cover photo by Kazuo Ogawa, Photonica, New York, New York

FINDING GOD WHERE YOU LEAST EXPECT HIM
Copyright © 2003 by John Fischer
Published by Harvest House Publishers
Eugene, Oregon 97402
www.harvesthousepublishers.com

Library of Congress Cataloging-in-Publication Data
Fischer, John, 1947-
  Finding God where you least expect him / John Fischer.
  p. cm.
  ISBN 0-7369-1058-1 (pbk.)
  1. Christian life. I. Title.
  BV4501.3.F57 2003
  248.4--dc21
                                                              2003001828

All rights reserved. No part of this publication may be reproduced, stored in a retrieval system, or transmitted in any form or by any means—electronic, mechanical, digital, photocopy, recording, or any other—except for brief quotations in printed reviews, without the prior permission of the publisher.

Printed in the United States of America.

03 04 05 06 07 08 09 10 11 / VP-KB / 10 9 8 7 6 5 4 3 2 1

"Everywhere I go I see you."

To the life and music of Rich Mullins,
who was always finding God.

Contents

ONE

Getting More of God in Your Life

I want to hold your hand.
THE BEATLES

❖ ❖ ❖

The year was 1964. The Beatles were taking the pop world by storm and "I Want to Hold Your Hand" was number one on the charts. I was a sophomore in high school, and at 16, I was in possession of the most coveted thing a 16-year-old can own—a driver's license. Our family car at the time was a 1957 Ford Fairlane. It had a V-8 Thunderbird engine with dual exhaust pipes, and although it was an automatic, if I drove around in low gear I could get a significant rumble going.

Like a typical teenager, I was into whatever was cool, and what was cool in Southern California in 1964 was customizing your car. Because this was the family car, my options were limited, but if I had a hot date, I would stop a block away from my house and remove the wide "V" on the trunk lid and the chrome grille over the round taillights. This gave the car a smoother look. The final touch was to reset all the automatic buttons on the radio to the local rock stations. I wasn't allowed to listen to rock music around the house, so everything had to be reset and replaced at the conclusion of my evening. I know this seems tame by today's standards, but I was a model evangelical kid, and this was rebel behavior by all accounts.

One summer night I returned to my car after a prayer meeting with the youth group I was active in at my church. The '57 Ford was customized for a cruise, but the hoped-for date to Bob's Big Boy after church had not materialized. I was alone—or so I thought. As I revved up the engine and throttled all eight cylinders, the radio came on where I had left it, and soon "I Want to Hold Your Hand" was bouncing happily over the airwaves. This time the song was met by an instinctive reaction to turn it off.

Our youth group had experienced an unusual closeness to God that particular night, and I entered my car bathed in a kind of spiritual glow. Given the cultural bent of my upbringing, I immediately felt that this music was a secular assault on my current state. This didn't mean I was going to stop listening to this music; it just didn't feel appropriate at that particular time when I felt so close to God. In my cultural theology and in my experience so far, God and rock and roll were antithetical. So I did what was instinctive. I reached to turn off the radio, but my hand never got to the knob.

Now I am usually a bit cynical about stories of God showing up in people's lives and saying this or that to them, so I would not pass on this story if I hadn't been convinced from the moment it happened that God was in the car with me, and both physically and spiritually interacted with me in ways I had not experienced before and haven't since. Point is, my hand was stopped by an invisible force, and I was suddenly aware that the music was not driving the presence of God away. I know I didn't make this up because this was such a shock to me. I had assumed that the Beatles and God could not possibly occupy the same space at the same time. In this case, that space was the inside of the car I was in. What happened next was a conversation in my head while the music played on. What I heard went something like this:

"Why are you turning off the music?"

"Well...I'm feeling very close to you," I replied.

"So?"

"Rock and roll is bad. It's supposed to take my mind off you."

"Is your mind off me right now?"

"No," I replied. "Not at all. In fact, I've never heard you more clearly."

"Good. So tell me honestly: What do you think about this music?"

I couldn't speak, fearing reprisal if I spoke the truth that I liked it. But then again, this was God, so he knew what I was thinking anyway.

"I like it."

"How does it make you feel?"

"Happy and free."

"How do I make you feel?"

"Happy..."

"And?"

"...and free."

"Well then, why don't you enjoy me and the music at the same time? Why don't you let your heart worship me? What's more, why don't you write me the music?"

For all intents and purposes, this was when I was called to serve God through music. "Write me the music" provided the drive that would carry me through 30 years of songwriting, singing, and recording what is now called contemporary Christian music. I was not alone in this pioneering effort, and I have found that others, who led the way with me into this new expression of faith, received a similar visitation around the same time.

But before this visitation was a call (I didn't really start writing the music until about four years later), it was a reeducation. It was the first time I saw God unthreatened by the small confines of my upbringing. This was the first time I saw God outside the evangelical box I had him in, and it was the beginning of a restructuring of my world-view—something that has been going on ever since.

If God was in the car with me that day, if he accepted my sing-along-with-the-Beatles as praise, if he could talk to me while the music played, if he actually prevented me from turning it off, then this is a God I want to get to know. This is a God who delights in being with me—a God who delights in what delights me. This could seriously alter one's worldview.

Reality Chasm

Most of us have a hard time imagining God is interested in half the stuff we are interested in. Hobbies, recreation, entertainment, and even our work seem outside his realm of concern, especially in what everyone would now agree is a secular society (as if society were ever anything but "secular"). The daily pursuits of our lives seem mundane in light of a Sunday morning worship service that leads us to focus on higher things. And so most of us ride on a perpetual seesaw between the sacred and the profane, and there is little encouragement from either side of this spiritual spectrum to embrace the other. When one is up, the other is down, and there is little teaching and fewer models of those who try to bring the two together. Those who try are suspect in both camps—too sacred for the sinners and too sinful for the saints.

Few people would say they are bent on doing evil. Almost everyone would say they want to do good and be a good person, while quickly qualifying that desire by noting how far they are from accomplishing this goal. If they claim to be a good person already, that claim would be relative to others who are not so good. A lot of these same people (the not-so-good ones) are put off by those who appear to be "together" or who wear the robes of religion. They suspect that with these people all is not what it seems. Indeed, scandals in the ranks of TV preachers and the exposure of pedophilic priests only confirm this assumption.

Because of these discrepancies, a chasm is often created in community where spirituality is a commodity—a kind of reality chasm, you might call it. Those who aspire to be more spiritual are often less believable than the sinners. The sinners are real and dirty; the saints are holy and aloof—often counting on their separation from the rest to foster a certain aura of righteousness. The big question of real Christianity is how to bridge this chasm. Can you bring God down without getting him dirty? Can you lift sinners up without making them phony?

This chasm exists not only in our perceptions of ourselves and others, but in the use of our time and the function of our pursuits. Certain activities are considered secular; others, sacred. Those who genuinely want to grow spiritually often find themselves in conflict between their desire for righteousness and the so-called secular demands on their time and interests. It is often held that this is why we need pastors and full-time church staff—so that we can pay them to spend the bulk of their time thinking about God and imparting to us, who have little time for such things, the results of their efforts. This thinking can even approach a kind of surrogate righteousness, where the pastor's holiness vicariously blankets everyone else in the church with a sort of purity by proxy. This might explain why the moral failure of a pastor is so devastating. If everyone in the congregation is cashing in on a pastor's spirituality, then his or her failure could be seen as a reflection of everyone else's bankruptcy of soul.

Stairway to Heaven or the Descent of God?

The most common means of bridging this gap is to dedicate more time and effort to God. Indeed, it is guilt over this moral disparity that drives people to church and to a periodic "rededication" of their lives to Christ. We promise God more of our time. We promise him better behavior. The average churchgoer feels that the exemplary Christian life is out there somewhere way beyond their grasp. Religious books, tapes, and seminars become steps on a self-help stairway to heaven.

Some give up.

The nonchurchgoer doesn't even want to try. She either feels the holy life is beyond her or she judges it all as being a superficial game.

So how do we bridge this gap? Meet halfway? Such is the nature of human arrogance to think we could even try. Since the earliest records of human beings on earth, there are biblical and extra-biblical stories of our attempts at this. Religious architecture always stretches upward. It seems basic to our existence to think God is somewhere in the air above our heads. Is this not why, in a religious context, that our eyes go up, our steeples go up, and our prayers go up? It does not appear to be a human invention to bring God down to our level; so it is left for us to try and rise to his—a rather dubious task, to say the least. That we even try is a testament to our stupidity and our pride in refusing to see ourselves as we really are.

This usually gets translated in a moral sense to a kind of human perfection. The person in the monastery, the cloister, the ivory tower is a person who has reached a level of moral achievement that puts him or her above the rest. In other writings I have called this "the big Christian lie"—the belief that someone, somewhere, is getting it right. Of course, no one knows anyone who is; we simply presume this person exists. As long as we believe someone out there is the perfect Christian, we can perpetuate the lie and legitimize all of our efforts to be that person. I suppose some might think their pastor qualifies for this, but that is only if they do not know their pastor very well. We have to believe and perpetuate the lie, otherwise we would have to give up on our own contrived righteousness (and the religious hucksters would be out of business). Isn't it a shame that our stubbornness keeps us pursuing what keeps us stubborn?

What if we all suddenly realized the big Christian lie for what it is? What would happen if we trusted the Scriptures after all? "There is no one righteous, not even one" (Romans 3:10). What would change? For one, it would be a big relief. It would even the score among us all, spiritually speaking. It would make acceptance by God based on God and not anything in us. It would put us all in the same boat. And finally, it would force us to find another way to bridge this gap. With even the best Christians living a lie, climbing up to meet God is out of reach to all but Jesus.

Perhaps it's time to take another look at bringing God down, but to do this we will have to adjust our thinking. Something about this sounds crude to our ears. We are used to a God who is up there, higher up than any of us are or want to be. Bringing God down sounds like we are besmirching his holiness, dragging him down to our level, dirtying his white robes in the foulness of our human experience.

But here is both the shocking and the glorious truth of the gospel. We didn't pull him down; he came down of his own accord. God is already down, and this is what makes the gospel so scandalous. As Robert Farrar Capon has put it, "The Bible, from Genesis to Revelation, has one Word for us: God has upped and done the damnedest thing. Or, to get the direction and adjectives right, God has downed and done the blessedest thing we could ever not have thought of."[1]

It is the sheer audacity of this that stands as one of the strongest proofs of the Bible and its account of the gospel: We simply never would have thought of God coming down. It is not in our intelligence to come up with this. Given the natural workings of the human mind, it is the utter preposterousness of the descent of God that is the gospel's strongest argument.

God came down, and in doing so, he has violated all our foolish attempts at our own holiness. God came down, and he stares at us eye to eye through "the least of these" in his own creation. He tore the veil off our spiritual pride. God came down, and it is a scandal that leaves us gloriously helpless when it comes to our own righteousness. He busted the big Christian lie wide open.

> In your relationships with one another, have the same attitude of mind Christ Jesus had: Who, being in very nature God, did not consider equality with God something to be used to his own advantage; rather he made himself nothing by taking the very nature of a servant, being made in human likeness. And being found in appearance as a human being, he humbled himself by becoming obedient to death—even death on a cross! (Philippians 2:5-8).

Bringing God Down

I hate playing blocks with my two-year-old. Our play always degenerates into a "knocking over" game. At first he tolerates my towers—even assists me in building them. (If you're wondering who's playing with whom, you're getting my point.) But it soon becomes apparent that his allowance is only for a limited time. Sooner or later the greater pleasure overrules, and he saunters over with that mischievous eye of his and down comes our masterpiece—well, my masterpiece that survived his collaboration. I always observe his patience shorten as this play continues. The towers get smaller and smaller until he is knocking down every block I set up, thus revealing the true nature of his interest in the game. His goal is not to build but to knock down. Where does this come from, I wonder? It seems uniquely human. I've noticed it with all my children. Perhaps it is some innate desire to level the playing field. To make all things equal.

God knocks down our self-induced spiritual blocks. No wonder so many people find religion so frustrating. On one hand, we think God exists somewhere up in the clouds, but when anyone tries to get to him, he knocks their tower down. Here's a brief summary of the history of religion: We build a tower; God knocks it down. We build another tower; God knocks it down. Etc., etc.

It is curious to me, in light of this discussion, to reflect on our mode of corporate worship in the church that seems to be centered mostly on putting God up. Our lyrics, our focus, is all up. We look up when we sing instead of down into our hymnals. We lift up our hands and lift up our praise, and this is all well and good—even biblical. But I wonder if there might be an ulterior motive to this. I wonder if there might be an element to our lifting up of God in weekly worship that is for the purpose of keeping him there—of sliding him up onto a shelf somewhere in our thinking where we can leave him when we walk out of church. This could be convenient. There might be certain advantages to not having God enter our world of daily life.

It is in this way that we need to bring God down. Not to besmirch him, but to bring him down in our thinking to where he connects with life for us at ground zero. And the reason we need to do this is because he is down already. We are not "bringing God down," we are merely bringing our thoughts into conformity with the truth. We are correcting our vision. We do not only look up to see God; we look across. We look over. We look inside and out. And then we look down to find him in those we judge, because, in truth, that's where he is most likely to be found.

Utopic Christians

Here's an interesting take on vision correction. I am near-sighted. The professional term for this degenerative condition is myopia. I can see fairly well up close, but I can't see well far away. It's a label that identifies a strength and leaves the assumption that the opposite is where the problem is. To put our spiritual state in similar terms, you could say we are "upsighted." Upsighted people can see God lifted up, but they can't see him down or across or in or out. Instead of myopia, I would call this "utopia." We only see God in the perfect.

Utopic Christians can't see God in the flawed, in the disappointment, in the poor, or in the unfinished quality of their lives—even in the average. They see him in the winners, not the losers. They see him in victory, not defeat. They are utopic Christians, only capable of worship when everything is supposedly perfect and we are all looking up.

If you can only see God when you look up, then faith will never meet your daily life. You can't walk around looking up all the time. You can't do your work well, and you run the chance of running into somebody or something because you are not paying attention to where you are going. We need a vision correction that allows us to pay attention to God and what we are doing at the same time. People who are nearsighted need lenses to help them see far away. People who are upsighted need lenses to help them see down, and in doing so, to see God down here. He is everywhere, all the time. This is where real faith begins: seeing God down...around...in...out...through...beyond...before...after...between...and in the middle of...everything.

Secular God

And what would those lenses need to do? First, they would change our understanding of God. If we could meet God for a casual chat, I wager we would find him interested in virtually anything. I think we'd find him pretty well read and up on current events. As a matter of fact, because of the huge variety of interests he has, he might appear to some Christians as a rather secular God.

Either God started the world in motion and slipped away to his holy heaven to let it run on its own, or he started it and stayed with it as a player—a participant in his own creation. This is certainly the biblical model and the reason for a triune God. The Father has an eye to and fro on the whole earth with nothing escaping his gaze (2 Chronicles 16:9 NASB). The Son walked here once in the flesh and knows what it is like to come from dust and return to it (Genesis 3:19). And the Holy

Spirit now indwells our flesh, going where we go, seeing what we see, and hearing what we hear—even praying for us when we cannot find the words for our emotions (Romans 8:26). That all sounds to me like a God who is pretty involved.

If God sees everything, wouldn't you want to know what he thinks about what he sees? I venture to guess he has an opinion; why don't we ask him about that? Do we walk out of a movie and wonder what God thought of it? Do we finish a fine meal and wonder if God liked it? Do we read the paper and wonder what God's take on the news is? Or better yet, do we find him in the news? We need to adopt a way of thinking that puts God within the frame of our daily vision.

Forty years ago, God busted in on my limited idea of him when he dropped in on me in my parents' '57 Ford. And he surprised me twice. First, I didn't expect him to be there (it's one thing to believe in your head that God is with you all the time; it's another thing to have him strike up a conversation with you in your car while listening to the Beatles), and second, I didn't expect him to be either knowledgeable of, or interested in, my musical tastes. So much for keeping God distant and in his heaven.

TWO

It's a Material World

...and I'm a material girl

MADONNA

❖ ❖ ❖

Only boys who save their pennies make Madonna's day. In her 1980s hit "Material Girl," pop singer Madonna extolled the virtues of brazen materialism. As much as she might like to dance and be romanced, at the end of the day it's the guy with the cold hard cash who ends up being Mr. Right. It's a material world she lives in, and in this song Madonna admits she is a material girl. Well, she's right about that. We live in a material world, and we are material people. This is, of course, not all that we are, but it is certainly an important part of the equation. And it is this material existence that has presented problems for Christians in every generation since Christ.

There has always existed, for the religious, a dichotomy between material and spiritual, flesh and spirit, body and soul, tangible and mystical. This dichotomy springs from an innate struggle with evil—not some evil force outside us, but the evil within. Paul's famous Romans 7 struggle with sin is common to us all and for that reason rings true. "So I find this law at work: Although I want to do good, evil is right there with me. For in my inner being I delight in God's law; but I see another law at work in me, waging war against the law of my mind and making me a prisoner of the law of sin at work in me. What a wretched man I am!" (Romans 7:21-24).

Indeed, all believers know the wretchedness of this struggle in some form or another. Our innermost being has been born again and rejoices in the truth. We want to do the right thing, but there is this other part of us that finds pleasure in seeking its own fulfillment apart from the good desires of the Spirit. If the great apostle Paul is caught in this struggle, then there is no way anyone else is going to escape it. We cry out with Paul, "Who will rescue me from this body of death?" (Romans 7:24). But unlike Paul, who goes on in the next breath to say "Thanks be to God, who delivers me through Jesus Christ our Lord!" (verse 25), we do not always go to God to be delivered. That's because we have other ways of dealing with this struggle, the most prevalent of which is to pretend it doesn't exist.

Let's face it. If there was a way to not have to deal directly and continually with one's sinful nature, don't you think we would all take it? I believe this is exactly the road most traveled, though not always acknowledged. This avoidance measure is done primarily by aligning the sinful nature entirely with our physical selves, or what the New Testament sometimes calls "the flesh." In so doing we can assume that everything that is wrong with us springs from the material world and our physical existence in it. Spirituality, as a result, becomes a mystical, out-of-body experience that relates very little to the world around us. It is a heavenly minded spirituality that owes its most treasured moments to that which leads one away from the clutches of the real world and its emphasis on the flesh. As such, it is more of an escape from the material world than any kind of presence in it.

In other words, the natural...physical...material...has become the whipping boy of a new gnostic Christianity, making the material world the culprit. By gnostic Christianity, I mean a faith that tries to avoid any connection between what we believe as Christians and how we actually live out our lives in the world. It's a kind of practical "disconnect" where the problem is not me, it's the flesh in me. This thinking separates the spiritual, taking it out of context with the physical and making God and good entirely mystical. Holiness becomes something out-of-body. Heck, we can even go as far as the gnostics of Jesus' day and disregard the whole physical world (our bodies included) when it comes to spiritual matters. It doesn't matter what we do in the material world or how we interact with it because what happens in the material world is irrelevant to spirituality. It only matters what we think, know, and believe. What we do is inconsequential. (Note how short a step it is from here to: It doesn't matter what we do six days a week as long as we are in church on Sunday making up for it all.) Like Madonna, we are living in a material world, but unlike her, we are not material people. We are spiritual people whose material existence is a kind of necessary evil. Out of convenience, Madonna unabashedly embraces the material to the exclusion of the metaphysical. Christians do the opposite but in the same manner. We reject the material world when convenient and absolve ourselves of responsibility in the real world.

I have always been susceptible to this kind of thinking because there are plenty of times I wouldn't mind making the world go away. I have been trained to see the world as a necessary evil, and my spirituality as far more important, and I have found this way of thinking useful to me even when I know it is wrong. If you walked into my office right now, you would find letters and bills piled high on my desk. I don't even have a spot for my laptop anymore. I have to put it on top of a pile and plug it in to use it temporarily. That's okay because I am only temporary anyway. Tomorrow I travel again and will leave all this behind, which is exactly what I would prefer to do because those piles represent questions I have no answers for and connections to the material world that make life uncomfortable for me. So I tell myself my ministry is the most important thing and justify leaving piles on my desk that undoubtedly contain things that put my family at risk.

Wouldn't it be nice if the following were true? We could go to church, worship God, and do as we please with the rest of our lives and still maintain a clear conscience. Is it any surprise that this explains much of Christian behavior today—going to church, worshiping God, and doing whatever we please with the rest of our lives? The polls and statistics continually point to this disconnection in areas such as divorce, child abuse, wife abuse, and premarital sex among Christians. How do we get away with this? By being gnostic Christians.

Gnosticism comes from the Greek word *gnosis* ("to know"), and its central tenant is that it matters only what you know in your head. If you believe the right things, you attain a higher state of intelligence. The material world relates to a lower form of intelligence and is ultimately of no consequence. Christians in today's Western culture are far more gnostic than anyone would realize or admit. We allow for this separation to exist because of the way it works for us.

The new gnosticism allows us to compartmentalize God, which creates a certain advantage for our sinful nature: We can be justified in leaving God out of a good deal of our daily lives. The thinking goes something like this:

1. Our physical existence is by nature sinful.

2. It cannot be avoided, however, because we all have to live in this skin and work here in this world.

3. We therefore can't expect too much of ourselves, spiritually. (This includes excusing a good deal of sin. After all, we're only human.)

4. We just have to try and spend more time with God and other Christians.

5. We have to count on professional Christians to be spiritual all the time and pass on their spiritual nuggets to us, while we muddle through the minefield of our decadent but unavoidable secular environment.

Like a God we do not bring down, our idea of holiness is a state of being untainted by the world or the flesh. And since this cannot be attained here on earth, we must learn to tolerate a certain duality in our thinking and practice. I am convinced that most Christians today live in two unconnected worlds. We think and do things in one world that are not consistent with what we do in the other. And because, as Madonna reminded us, the material world dominates over everything else, we of necessity possess a spirituality that is marginal in relation to the world we occupy—more like a dangling participle in a world of verbs that drive our thought and action at all times.

A Material God

The real problem here is that we have no theology for being human. The material world eats up most of our attention, and because our idea of faith is so very uncomfortable in a material world, it loses in the end. The average Christian is caught embracing a dubious physical existence while desperately, and with limited success, trying to hold onto a faith that is antithetical to it.

The tragedy in having no theology for being human is that the Bible, from Genesis to Revelation, is all about one thing: birthing, losing, and saving the human race—a story where being human plays a pretty central role. The Bible's core message is about how God created, redeemed, and ratified the human predicament by becoming human himself. This in itself is the greatest affirmation our material world could ever receive from God—that he could actually take on our flesh and live in this material world himself. Move over Madonna. God created a material world for us to live in, and if he came and lived in it, then we must deduce that he is, among other things, a material God.

So where does this come from—this separation between flesh and spirit, this duality between body and soul—if it is not biblical? If God is a material God, then why do we not think of him as such?

It's All Greek to Me

I remember how much of a shock it was to my system when I first realized this dualistic philosophy was not biblical. The profaneness of our fleshly state and worldly environment was so ingrained in the Christianity I inherited from a fundamental evangelical background that I never questioned it. That's why I was startled to find its origin more in the thinking and writings of Plato and Aristotle than in any biblical texts. The Romans may have ruled politically in Jesus' day, but the Greeks ruled in thought and worldview, and much of that worldview distorted early Christianity and is still coloring our thinking to this day. One can see how a Greek philosophy that gave preference to the spiritual realm and cast doubt on the physical could easily mix with Paul's teaching on flesh and Spirit and push it to a level of gnosticism where there is nothing good about the physical and nothing physical about Christ.

There is power in a dualistic way of thinking that may explain its stubbornness. Gnosticism legitimizes hypocrisy. It makes it irrelevant how you live, because to the gnostic, the physical realm is an illusion anyway. One can see how the gnostic approach neatly solves Paul's dilemma between his inner being that delights in God's law and the law of sin at work in his mortal flesh. It simply cancels out one side of the equation. It nullifies our human existence. Gnostic thinking puts spirituality on a separate plane where it does not have to interact with the physical consequences of our everyday lives. And we love that about it.

The Fifth Gospel

McNair Wilson is an actor, playwright, author, lecturer in creativity, and personal friend and entertainer of my children, who, in the mid-1970s, created a 90-minute one-act play on the life of Christ using nothing more for props than a trunk and a broom. In this brilliant play called *The Fifth Gospel,* Jesus is presented as a human being. His divinity is definitely apparent and implied, but it is his human side that is explored with humor and spunk. Some of the stories acted out are true to the biblical text—the healing of a blind man, the razing of the temple, the humiliation of the Pharisees, and the pain and glory of the crucifixion and resurrection. Other stories come from Wilson's imagination—the boy Jesus who used his newly discovered miraculous power to magically complete his household chores, the adolescent Jesus falling in love with Elizabeth at the annual temple bazaar, or the adult Jesus indulging in a water fight with his disciples (Matthew won). These situations are obviously imaginary, but they get the traditional evangelical mind to truly face up to the possibilities of a human Jesus. You realize that if these things didn't happened, something like them did.

I have personally witnessed this play performed to scores of audiences everywhere from living rooms to large theaters, and every show I've witnessed has been to a mostly evangelical audience which visibly struggled with encountering such a human Christ. Wilson knows the themes he presents are radical, so he always includes as part of the show a question-and-answer session at the conclusion of each performance to help people grapple with these concepts. Every one of those sessions revealed a group of people who have given very little thought to a human Christ. They also revealed a strong resistance to wanting such a Christ. This alone is strong evidence of a prevalent gnostic Christianity.

And this human rendition of the divine is not only a stretch for believers. More popular presentations, such as *Godspell, Jesus Christ Superstar,* and the much-criticized *Last Temptation of Christ,* present us with a human Jesus, and even unbelievers are captured by the idea. What this indicates, among other things, is a flaw in both the way Christ is usually presented and the way he is most often perceived. That's because it is such a radical idea in relationship to typical religious thinking to envision Christ as fully human. But Jesus, of necessity, must be fully human and fully divine. Without a fully human Jesus, we are not fully saved. How far away are we from true Christianity when the humanity of the Son of Man—truly the core of the Christian message—is shown to be such a novel idea to those who are supposedly his followers?

Nonnegotiables

It is essential to our real life in a real world that Jesus Christ came in the flesh and died on a real wooden cross, was buried in a real tomb located somewhere outside the city of Jerusalem, and rose again, to be seen and touched by those who knew him and walked with him for three years prior. If the physical realm is real, and we must answer to God for what we do in it, then we're cooked without a human Christ, because we are all real sinners in a real world. This is why Christ on the cross both condemns and saves us. The cross condemns us in our sin—it agrees that sin is real and a price must be paid for indulging in it—but it saves us through Christ's perfect atonement for our sin (though he was human and knew temptation, still he knew no sin in his life except for our sin, which was laid upon him in his final hours on the cross) and his resurrection seals our salvation, giving us ultimate power over death.

But if Christ be not physical, then we are not saved.

This is why today's Christian must guard against any thinking that would exempt Christ from the total human experience. John the apostle is so strong on this that he stated unabashedly in his first New Testament letter that "Every spirit that acknowledges that Jesus Christ has come in the flesh is from God, but every spirit that does not acknowledge Jesus is not from God. This is the spirit of the antichrist" (1 John 4:2-3). Notice that it is not enough to acknowledge Jesus (the gnostics could do that) but a particular Jesus is the one John is talking about here—the one who came in a flesh-and-blood body. The material Jesus. God in a human body. This is a nonnegotiable aspect of biblical theology; it is critical to our salvation. If Jesus was not God in human form, then his death and resurrection cannot touch our humanity. He can pay the price for somebody, maybe, but not us. Without a material Jesus, we are all dead in our trespasses and sins.

One of Us

If Madonna extolled a material world, another female artist, Joan Osborne, sang a surprisingly popular song in the 1990s that at least raised the question of God doing this very thing—coming to the material world as "one of us." In "One of Us" she has God coming to our postmodern world as a "slob" like one of us and a stranger on a bus just trying to find his way home. The success of this song as a mainstream hit shows how the scandalous nature of the incarnation continues to captivate Christians and non-Christians alike.

The song was written by a former member of a one-hit Philadelphia band and recorded by a brassy, irreverent feminist with marginal success until it boosted her into the limelight. What makes this story so compelling is the fact that neither one of these people, by their own admission, knew what they were doing in the creation of this song.

"I never thought about any of it," said the writer, Eric Bazilian, about the lyrics of "One of Us" in a *Washington Post* story. "I just take credit for being the scribe. This song knows what it's saying even though I don't. Whoever dictated this piece knew where it was going."[1] And the singer, Joan Osborne, confirmed the mystery: "We have this theory that this song is a living creature with a mind of its own that used Eric to be born and used me to spread its message throughout the world."[2]

What's even more amazing is how "One of Us" slipped out into popular culture under the radar of Christian music and a Christian subculture. It was, in fact, largely rejected by

Christians as blasphemy that made God into a slob, ridiculed his greatness and goodness, and had the pope as the only one ringing up heaven on the phone. There are definitely large doses of humor and irony in the song, and a certain ambivalence and possible offense to conservative Christians that probably helped carry it into the mainstream market. But its central message is hard to ignore, especially the second verse, which carries the bold challenge that if we could actually see God's face in human form, we would then have to believe the whole story, including heaven, Jesus, the saints, and the prophets.

Jesus once put his disciples on the spot by asking them the same question, "Who do you say I am?" to which Peter, in no uncertain terms replied, "You are the Christ, the Son of the living God" (Mark 8:29; Matthew 16:16). "One of Us" takes that answer a step further. If Jesus was the Son of God and "one of us"—what would that mean?

Here are some possibilities:

1. It would mean God would understand us through identification with our material existence.

2. It would mean our human experience could be touched by the divine. If Jesus walked this earth and lived a sanctified life in our flesh and blood, then at least the possibility is there that we can experience this same life as well.

3. It would mean all of life could be sacred.

4. It would mean that, in Christ, the spiritual and the physical meet, forever sounding the death knell on gnostic Christianity.

5. It would mean that God is a lot more involved in our physical world than we think.

God was certainly more involved with the world of popular culture if we assume he influenced the creation of this song; and if we take the direct testimony of the songwriter and the singer, he did. If the writer and the singer of a song about the incarnation of Christ absolve themselves of responsibility in its creation, then where else could its inspiration lie than with the Holy Spirit? Making God responsible for the creation and success of a popular song is a stretch for some people's theology but no problem for a God who knows no physical bounds. All this is to affirm that life in the physical realm and in a physical body can and should be touched by the presence and spirit of Christ, who once walked this earth in human form as the "Son of Man" and now not only indwells all who believe in him, but can also influence and speak through those who don't.

Good Flesh

Brian Wren is a contemporary hymn writer whose lyrics appear in a Christmas cantata titled *Welcome All Wonders*. His lyrics are arresting in the fact that they directly refer to what is good about the flesh we all live in. In a clever restructuring of John's declaration "the Word became flesh" (John 1:14), Wren has constructed the scandalous lyric: "Good is the flesh that the Word has become" in one of the five pieces in this ambitious choral/orchestral work. It stands to reason that if the Word became flesh, then flesh, by association at least with Christ, must be good. It is a self-evident truth. And yet to even say the words "good" and "flesh" in the same sentence creates a huge obstacle for most Christians. This proves once again, the gnostic nature of much current Christianity. This song would not be scandalous if Christians were currently embracing what is good about their own human existence.

The negative reaction to this lyric has been confirmed by the creator of the cantata, J.A.C. Redford, who attests to the many comments he inevitably receives from evangelical audiences who question the theology of "good flesh." With his gracious permission, let's visit Brian Wren's lyric for a moment.

> Good is the flesh that the Word has become
>   good is the birthing, the milk in the breast,
>   good is the feeding, caressing and rest,
>   good is the body for knowing the world,
> Good is the flesh that the Word has become.[3]

The theological question at hand is whether Christ's good experience in the flesh was possible only because of his sinless nature and not accessible to us because of our sin. Flesh is often used in Scripture in a spiritual sense as the whole person organized in the wrong direction. But flesh can also simply mean that which is physical. Paul talks about those who have not seen him "in the flesh" as meaning those who have not yet met him personally—no implication of sin at all (Colossians 2:1 KJV). And Paul, the one famous for presenting the lusts and desires of the flesh that enslave us, also claimed that the life he lived "in the flesh" he lived by faith (Galatians 2:20 KJV). This would seem to put Christ's good life in the flesh as available to us also by faith. Christ becoming human elevates the state of our existence and brings a sacred presence to our natural human lives.

> Good is the body for knowing the world,
>   sensing the sunlight, the tug of the ground,
>   feeling, perceiving, within and around,
>   good is the body, from cradle to grave,
> Good is the flesh that the Word has become.[4]

This is a rare statement of a Christian worldview with a wide angle on truth. "Good is the body for knowing the world" contains two disturbing thoughts for the evangelical mind: 1) our bodies are good for something and 2) there is good in the world to be known. In a learned environment where sex is bad and the world is evil, either of these concepts would meet with immediate skepticism.

Butch Hancock, a country/folk singer/songwriter who grew up in the Bible Belt, made fun of this skepticism by joking, "We grew up with two main things: God loves you and he's gonna send you to hell, and that sex is bad and dirty and nasty and awful and you should save it for the one you love."[5] The humor wouldn't be there if the sentiment wasn't widespread. This is the nature of popular evangelical thinking that casts doubt on the entire human experience.

The Tug of the Earth

So here we are in God's image with the divine pulling upward and the earth pulling down. That "tug of the ground" is not what makes us dirty; it's what keeps us here on this planet, rooted in earth, part of God's creation. It is what keeps us from flying off into vague spiritual mysticism. The tug of earth keeps what is spiritual rooted in what is physical. We resist this because we have not made peace with our bodies. We are too busy blaming and shaming our bodies to find and enjoy being spiritual in them. Many do not even know or believe this is possible.

This is why we have a hard time seeing the Lord Jesus in a human body. We're offended by every movie that has tried to put him in one. We don't like any of the artists who have tried to paint him. We don't imagine him that way. We imagine him a spirit in heaven, at the right hand of God, but fail to remember that he is embodied there as well. Yes, in a resurrected body, but a body still—recognized on earth by those who knew him, and recognizable in heaven by the same.

Few Christians today would realize or admit that the beliefs they hold about the humanity of Christ are less than biblical. Though we hold to biblical beliefs, in practice we are in some ways closer to New Age mysticism than true incarnation. Why? Because incarnation means getting down and getting human. Getting down and getting real. Getting down and climbing inside our skin, a place where most of us, if truth be known, are not very comfortable.

The body can be good, and the world can be known and embraced by the Christian without compromise. Our body provides the senses by which we know and encounter reality outside ourselves. Our eyes, ears, taste, touch, and smell interact daily with this sensuous experience of life. If God gave us these senses, then we are sensuous. Once again our bias against the physical is evident. Jesus saw, heard, tasted, touched, and smelled the world around him without sin. We need to reclaim what is good about our interaction with the physical world through our senses. My computer thesaurus comes up with 13 synonyms for "sensuous," and every one except for possibly "delicious" has a predominantly negative connotation. Words like "carnal," "hedonistic," and "erotic" prevail, and this is not even a Christian computer! If we are made in God's image, and God gave us five senses in which to experience the world around us, then these can all have a legitimate use in participating in what is good in the world.

> *Good is the body, from cradle to grave,*
>   *growing and aging, arousing, impaired,*
>   *happy in clothing, or lovingly bared,*
>   *good is the pleasure of God in our flesh,*
> *Good is the flesh that the Word has become.* [6]

Here is where, I am sure, the poet loses even those who might have stuck with him so far. Here he has us naked, aroused, and unashamed.

Most Christians carry their sexuality around as if it were a huge burden—one big temptation they wish they could live without. We have become so focused on the wrong use of the sex drive that we have become incapable of finding much right about it. Was being naked and unashamed reserved only for the garden? Was the gate forever closed on this vulnerable goodness? Do we conceive our offspring in shame and darkness and hope for early release from these terrible sins?

"Marriage should be honored by all, and the marriage bed kept pure" implies a purity in sex available to believers in marriage (Hebrews 13:4). One can only "keep pure" that which was pure to begin with. It's the adulterer and pornographer who defiles the marriage bed, not sex. As in much of our life on earth, we can become so preoccupied fighting what is bad that we fail to affirm what is good. Indeed, it will be through affirming what is good about the flesh that we will be better able to reject what is not.

Did Jesus merely tolerate his brief stay on earth? Was this incarnation just a dirty job somebody had to do (and good thing it was God), or did he actually enjoy it? Can you picture Christ enjoying his life on earth? Can you see him laughing or smiling or bright-eyed? Can you see him tired or frustrated or angry? We worship a God who is all powerful and all-knowing, a Son who is fully human, and a Spirit who is fully present, moving about this earth in our human bodies and interacting with us if we would only open our eyes to him.

Those are revolutionary words: the Word made flesh. Christ came in the flesh, and in doing so, announced to us all that the flesh is not the problem. Our humanity is not the problem. Our material existence is not the problem. God is not going to do away with our humanity and turn us all into odd-looking Martians or wisps of spiritual ghosts floating around the universe. No, he's redeeming us body, soul, and spirit. He wants the whole thing. He's even going to incorporate some of our ideas into his heaven, like streets and walls and cities and mansions. The grand experiment of creating people—male and female—in his image worked. There is nothing wrong with the package; it's just that sin twisted its focus away from God and onto ourselves. Redemption in Christ through his death and resurrection can reestablish our focus and put us right with ourselves and the world around us.

THREE

Hide-and-Seek

The secret things belong to the LORD...

DEUTERONOMY 29:29

❖ ❖ ❖

For anyone in the proximity of a television screen on September 11, 2001, the image of two of the tallest buildings in the world, with thousands of people trapped inside them, disintegrating in seconds into a mass grave of twisted metal and an empty sky is indelibly etched on the mind. And of all the questions that flooded the consciousness of a nation that day, the most vexing was: "Where was God when this happened?"

Where is God in the tragic events of life? Where is God in the mundane? Where is God, for that matter, in the day-to-day? I actually think it is easier to answer that question in relation to the tragic than it is to the average. That is because the cross always looms over the tragic.

The most poignant statement of 9/11 for me was brought home by a number of photos taken at ground zero by a pastor of our church who was allowed to gain access there two weeks after the attack. Sitting straight up in the air in one of those photos, as if erected by rescue crews bent on giving proper due to the missing dead, was a cross. This was not the cross we have since all seen on television and in photos that was constructed out of the rubble. No one put this cross together. No one put this cross there. It fell that way—sheered off from the blast into

35

perfect proportion and impaled straight into the wreckage from who knows how many stories up.

That was remarkable enough, but closer scrutiny of the other photos from the site revealed crosses everywhere, lying every which way, but perfectly cut as if an iron worker had been on assignment to create memorials for the dead. In one picture alone I counted eight perfectly proportioned crosses. The answer to where God was couldn't be clearer. He was right there in the middle of the carnage. He left his signature in the rubble.

No one who died in the collapse of the World Trade Center died alone. God died too. He died with them. He knows the pain, the fear, the agony. He took all that on—and more—on the cross. He also knows the loss of those who remain, having lost his beloved friend Lazarus. Yes, he brought Lazarus back from the dead, but that doesn't mean he didn't feel the loss and identify with the rest of us who are helpless in the face of death. He wept over this (John 11:35).

We are faced with a great irony. The tragedies that force us to ask, "Where was God when this happened?" are also the very things that get us asking, seeking, and knocking on heaven's door. Anyone will agree that America was more spiritually inclined in the days following 9/11 than in the days prior. Imagine trying to organize a "Where's God?" campaign on September 10, 2001, and guess how far you'd get. Ask "Where's God?" and you are likely to get as an answer: "Who cares?" But ask "Where's God?" after 9/11, and you have a ready audience.

More importantly and more illusive in our daily lives is: Where is God on all the other days? Where was God after things settled down, when the stock market came back up and our lives returned to some kind of normal, even if only an illusion of normalcy? In my experience these are the hardest times to find God, or more accurately, to be aware of him. The question needs to be rephrased. Not "Where was God?" but "Where is God? Where is he now? How can I find him?"

The Never-Ending Game

In the beginning God and the first couple took walks together in the garden. It was a perfect union. There was complete openness. The guileless nakedness of the man and woman reflected the transparency of their minds and hearts. Nothing was hidden. No secrets. Perfect communion. Right up until the devil's bargain. Then everything changed.

"Then the man and his wife heard the sound of the LORD God as he was walking in the garden in the cool of the day, and they hid from the LORD God among the trees of the garden. But the LORD God called to the man, 'Where are you?' " (Genesis 3:8-9). Thus began the longest hide-and-seek game in history. The game is as long as the human race is old. The first time, we hid. Then it was God's turn, and we've been hiding from each other—and seeking each other—ever since.

Last night we played hide-and-seek in bed—my wife, our three-year-old, and I. Marti and Chandler would go under the covers and I would go off looking all over the bedroom— under the bed, behind the hutch, behind the door, even in the next room—all the while calling out, "Where are you guys?" Then I would eventually want to know what the big bump in the middle of the bed was and grab Chandler's leg, to his squeals of delight. It's inexpressible, the look on his face when he pulls the covers down from his eyes and reveals himself. Anyone with any experience at this game knows that children never tire of it. Adults simply wear out. On one hand it seems so elementary, and I realize how brief the time will be until he rolls his eyes at this silly sport; but on the other hand it seems so true.

This is one of those moments when the child's view is the most accurate. This must be the way this exercise looks to God, because we are just as obvious to him as my wife and son are hiding under the covers. And yet he cries out, "Where are you?" Do we answer him? Are we overjoyed to be found like my three-year-old with bright eyes of amazement, or are we too old for this game?

At one point in our play I announced I was giving up on the search. My wife became so insistent against that idea that she shocked me. "Oh, no you're not! What would happen if God gave up on us?"

Thank goodness God didn't give up on Adam and Eve. He went looking for them and called to them under the covers, though their uncovering was not one of joy, but of shame.

Playing Hard to Get

It is important to see that this estrangement between God and the first couple was two-way. It broke up an intimate relationship and deprived God of us and us of God. We think more about us being deprived of God than we do about God being deprived of us. That's because we fail to remember that God values this relationship as much, if not more, than we do. He misses those walks in the garden, and he has arranged it so that he could bring us back into fellowship with him. We each want it, and need it, though need is a different thing for him than for us. For him, this relationship is his pleasure; for us, it is life and death. We actually are the desperate ones. We should be seeking him, even throwing ourselves at him, but we are full of pride.

True love is not desperate. No one wants to respond to someone waiting to smother them with needs. There is respect in a good relationship that we sometimes call "playing hard to get." It sounds like a manipulation—and sometimes it is—but it is not necessarily so. It is also a way of judging character and testing one's resolve. A person who is overwhelmed with their own need will most likely go find someone else to exploit, should they find their first source unresponsive. A real lover will persist.

True love is patient. It will wait. It can love from a distance, if need be. God's love is like this. He has been courting us throughout human history, but he does not throw himself at us. He said, "Do not give dogs what is sacred" (Matthew 7:6). To be sure, God will never become dog food in that way.

A relationship of respect gives room for response. Love cannot be forced. It cannot be commanded. But wait a minute: Isn't it the great commandment? Yes, but "Thou shalt love the Lord thy God..." can also look like "Thou shalt do the easiest thing there is to do once thou knowest how much thou art loved. Thou shalt love back. Thou shalt come into my embrace and taste my joy forever." "Oh, dear...well, let me think about this a minute." (That's what my wife said to me when I asked her to marry me—the longest minute in the world.)

Love gives, but love also holds back. That's what I see God doing. He loves us—has loved us to the cross, has done everything necessary to get us back—but he holds back too. He offers us salvation, but he does not force it on us. We don't have to respond. Don't forget this was a two-way relationship in the beginning. It still is, albeit an estranged one. But God is still the lover, still the pursuer; he just does it sometimes in the background, in the shadows. He is not obvious about his advances. He plays hard to get. He can be coy sometimes. And he still calls out to us, "Where are you?"

God Hides

Our hiding from God is easy to understand because of our sin, but his hiding from us is another story, a principle evident throughout the history of our race. In the Old Testament, he hid his face from Moses. He hid from the people, and he even had Moses veil his face to hide the residual glory that clung there from being in his presence. He shrouded himself in a pillar of fire by night and a cloud by day. Then he hid in the Ark of the Covenant (the ultimate God-in-a-box!). Later it was the prophets who divulged his words—often rejected by the people—as he became more and more obscure due to their unbelief. The mystery continued on into the New Testament, when the coming of God to earth was missed by all but a few shepherds and a handful of stargazing wise men following their astrological calculations. His true identity remained an enigma as he led a small group of ragamuffin believers under the noses of the elite religious establishment of the day. He died, relatively unknown, as a common criminal under the sign "King of the Jews," mocking an earthly greatness seemingly never realized. He was not promoted among the masses. His true identity was revealed only to a few. He performed the miraculous and then swore those who experienced his healing power to secrecy. And the security guards around his tomb slept through the most spectacular of all his amazing deeds—his own resurrection from the dead.

Following this, in a manner that captures metaphorically how God has dealt with human beings over the course of history, he walked and talked with two of his former disciples as a stranger explaining to them through the Scriptures everything about himself, and then he vanished moments after revealing himself to them, leaving them flush with a burning heart (Luke 24:13-32).

Why would he do this? Why would God be so bent on giving us only glimpses of his glory? Is it not because he is simply too great and glorious to be obvious? God defies definition. He cannot be contained. He is a grand paradox to be contemplated, not a doctrine to be espoused. He refuses to fit anywhere.

God hides because he would be too big to miss otherwise. Well then, why doesn't he make himself obvious so everyone can see him and believe? They would believe, wouldn't they? This is the same question posed by the song "One of Us" in the last chapter: Would you really want to see God if it meant you would have to believe in him? God hides precisely because he knows all will not believe, even if they could see. Seeing doesn't always mean believing. The Pharisees saw Jesus, and it didn't seem to do them any good. They saw him, heard him, had him over for dinner, and still they did not believe.

God's obscurity saves his integrity and the integrity of the unbeliever. The unbeliever can refuse to believe without looking like a fool. God has left room in his universe for credible unbelief. If God were obvious—if he could be seen by all as who he really is—no one would be able to not believe, and in a world that allows for unbelief, that would hardly be fair. As it is, God has so arranged it that believers look like fools. This foolishness in the world tests the strength and validity of a believer's faith. If you were a fool for not believing, you might believe reluctantly, or believe for the wrong reasons. If you are a fool for believing, and you believe anyway, it confirms the tenacity and reality of your faith. No one would knowingly look like a fool if they didn't want to or have to.

God has too much integrity and too much holiness to be taken lightly, so he hides as much for our protection as for his honor and worth. And I suppose some of our honor and worth is in this equation as well. God honors us to the extent that he gives us freedom to believe what we want, when we want to. God honors our choice and our free will. He wants us to choose him, and in order to have us choose him, there will of necessity have to be a real choice—something to choose from, and some who will choose something else and be just as happy or just as successful, at least for a while.

I used to ridicule the Frank Sinatra classic "I Did It My Way" as the theme song of hell. I see it now as actually a song that indirectly gives God glory. God created us and gave us the autonomy to do this—to sing about and celebrate our independence. This is a huge privilege. That it can lead to hell is not a condemnation of the freedom, but a tragedy of the will. That someone of such value, worth, and dignity could go away from God with head held high is a testament as much to God as it is to humanity, however fallen we are.

And so God is here, and he is not. He is here to some and not to others. He is under every rock, behind every bush, around every corner for some, and not anywhere to be found for others, even if they scaled the highest mountain or plunged into the deepest sea, or looked right at him—into his eyes—the way the Pharisees did.

"Be ever hearing, but never understanding," God said to Isaiah in a passage quoted later by Jesus. "Be ever seeing, but never perceiving. Make the heart of this people calloused; make their ears dull and close their eyes. Otherwise they might see with their eyes, hear with their ears, understand with their hearts, and turn and be healed" (Isaiah 6:9-10).

Jesus quoted this Isaiah passage when speaking of why he talked in parables (Matthew 13:14-16). He said that some would see and understand him while others would not. And in order to protect the truth from those who won't see it and reveal it to those who will, he chose to speak to them in parables. So he came in disguise and told stories only those who had ears to hear could understand. He chose the lowliest things to confound the wise. God went undercover and carried on a conspiracy for which he was finally crucified.

We Seek

Over the years this has come to be my favorite verse: "It is the glory of God to conceal a matter; to search out a matter is the glory of kings" (Proverbs 25:2). Now this probably comes as a surprise from someone who grew up with the truth being proclaimed in his home and in his church all the time. Why would I glory in a message of searching for God when I've seemingly known where he was all along?

I think I like this verse so much because, in fact, I haven't known where he was all along. I knew he was in the church and in the Bible and in the Christian things my family always did, but I used to think that was it. These were the only places to find God. It wasn't until I began to realize God could be found outside these things—indeed, it was outside of these things that I found him most real—that this verse began to take on such significance. It started inside a '57 Ford and then worked out from there. As soon as I found out God likes hiding, I started looking for him everywhere. And the more I looked, the more I found, until I began to realize this wasn't about his hiding as much as it was about my seeking. If we are looking, we will be finding. If we aren't looking for him, we will simply not find him. And what a tragedy that is, when he is right there, all the time. God wants us to "seek him and perhaps reach out for him and find him, though he is not far from any one of us" (Acts 17:27).

Ever notice that with a small child something hidden is always more intriguing than something found? In spite of what they say, the two birds in the bush are far more interesting than the one in the hand. It's a little like that with God. He lures us into the mystery. His concealment is an invitation to find out. And like a good father, at the right time, he brings what was hidden out into full view. He does not always frustrate us. It's the way it has always been: God hides; we seek.

Larry Wall, a Christian and creator of the Perl computer programming language, in response to a sarcastic Internet interview question about his self-proclaimed faith in God, replied:

> I take it to mean that you find it more or less inconceivable that someone with a scientific mind (or at least technical mind...) could choose to believe in God. I'd like to at least get you to the point where you find it conceivable. I expect a good deal of the problem is that you are busy disbelieving a different God than the one I am busy believing in...Please allow me to quote a couple "bits" from Hebrews, slightly paraphrased: You can't please God the way Enoch did without some faith, because those who come to God must (minimally) believe that: A) God exists, and B) God is good to people who really look for him.[1]

There it is. Take it from a computer programmer, who, according to his interviewer, shouldn't be believing. The key element in knowing God is to look for him. "Seek and you will find" (Matthew 7:7) is the way Jesus put the invitation, and it was just that—an invitation, not a command (remember, this is a relationship with give-and-take and a freedom of choice). It's an invitation with a promise.

Back to Proverbs 25:2, "...to search out a matter is the glory of kings." There are two kinds of glory in this verse. God's glory and ours. His glory is found in concealing things; ours is found in seeking them out. It is honorable and common to the activity of kings to search things out. (Remember those kings who sought out the Christ child?) Anybody who sets out on this journey to find God is counted noble.

This is what is commonly called liberal arts in most schools. The Hebrew word translated "matter," as in "to search out a matter," is as broad as it is long. It can mean "truth," it can mean "words," it can mean "things," or it can mean "anything." The implication is that there is something about God hidden everywhere, and in searching out virtually anything, something about him can be found.

This is not Christian education. This is not Sunday school material or Gospel Light curriculum. This is all of learning: everything contained in universities, everything in current events, and everything in popular culture as well as every experience life has to offer. In all of this, something about God is waiting to be found and experienced. God has hidden truths about himself in the matters of the universe and right down to the matters of our day.

God at Harvard

In the early formation of this country—in its first institutions of higher learning—it was thought of as a Christian thing to study philosophy, science, math, and the arts. God used to be at Harvard; now you seem to find him only at church or in a Christian bookstore. God has been seriously demoted in our institutions of higher learning. What a shame, because of course he is still at Harvard, as much as he ever was—it's just that most people don't find him there precisely because they aren't looking for him there.

In 1992, Ari L. Goldman, an Orthodox Jew, published *The Search for God at Harvard*. Though I have not personally read this book, it looks to be an excellent study on comparative religions with rather ambiguous conclusions. Five years later Harvard chaplain Kelly Monroe compiled another book entitled *Finding God at Harvard,* containing personal testimonies of Christian students, faculty, and former students who found a personal relationship with the God of the Bible while they were at Harvard.

So is God to be found at Harvard? It all depends on whom you ask.

Does this mean if you don't seek you won't find? As it relates to God, I believe it does. If God is hidden, how will anyone find him unless they look for him? There are no God-indicators popping up in various places. There are no labels on sacred things. Finding God is a factor of two things: the person doing the searching and God's will in revealing himself. There are no guarantees. You don't go to "God school" to get this. You seek and you pray and you seek some more. Pretty soon your whole life is bent on seeking.

Herein lies the challenge. I would venture to put forth that not many Christians—or those who claim to be Christians—are actively seeking God in their daily lives. They are not finding God as much as they could because they are not looking for him. Many Christians find it adequate enough to have God in the God compartment of their lives, and they don't go looking for him anywhere else. They already found God. They have the God-thing solved. It's a wrap. They worship on Sundays, they pray to him in their devotions, and when they are really in trouble they call on him in the middle of the day, but the rest of their lives are lived in a world where, for all practical purposes, he doesn't exist. He wouldn't like it anyway, or so they think. The world as they see it is unsuitable for God, but a necessary evil for them. It is a bad place for the holy, certainly a place God would want to avoid.

Thinking like this is merely a projection on God of our own feelings and fears about the world. Since we as Christians don't like the world, we assume God doesn't like it either. Otherwise our beliefs would be in conflict, which is exactly the case for many Christians. Too few Christians actually realize their view of the world is often at odds with God's.

Where Do You Seek?

It is my belief that the rise of a Christian subculture in America has had an adverse effect on the ability of Christians to seek God and find him as a standard practice in their daily lives. The more acculturated a person is into the Christian subculture, the more suspect the wider world becomes. And anyway, if Christian things have all been gathered together in one place, why look any further? Why subject myself to secular society when I don't have to?

That which is Christian is already arranged neatly on the shelves of the local Christian bookstore. If a Christian version of virtually every aspect of popular culture is now readily available through Christian retailing, looking for God anywhere else seems irrelevant. Why go to community aerobics and put up with offensive lyrics when you can go to aerobics at the church and work out to Christian music? Why go into Barnes and Noble when everything necessary for your Christian life, growth, and even entertainment is available at the Christian bookstore? Why pay for the experience of sitting through foul language and gratuitous sex just to try and find something good in a popular movie? Why—when good, wholesome Christian entertainment is available—would anyone do such a thing?

To understand where thinking like this comes from, we will take a look at contemporary Christian culture and thinking through a historian's eye. It's revealing and somewhat shocking to find out how much those outside our subculture know about us. In her landmark work, *Material Christianity: Religion and Popular Culture in America*, Colleen McDannell observed the following:

> Scholars and the media have documented theological battles between conservative and liberal

Protestants, the rise and fall of televangelists, and the political influence of the Religious Right. They have paid little attention, however, to the everyday lives of white, politically conservative, and fundamentalist Christians. These Christians are no longer exclusively poor, rural and Southern. Instead, they are found throughout American society. To varying degrees, these Christians attempt to interact only with those who share their religious life styles while at the same time trying to "right" both American society and individual Americans. They send their children to private schools or, increasingly, teach them at home. They live in the suburbs but their children do not watch television or go to popular movies. With their non-Christian neighbors they are friendly but rarely best friends. Churchgoing goes far beyond an hour on Sunday morning. Christian telephone books give them the names and numbers of Christian dentists, cruise companies, therapists, and plumbers. When they want to rent a video, learn how to cope with a divorce, or buy a wedding present, they go to a Christian bookstore.

Being Christian means to have a Christian life style that includes purchasing goods from a fellow Christian and using those goods. The stress that is placed on critically thinking about religion in liberal traditions holds less importance in conservative Christianity than doing religious activities and identifying oneself as Christian.[2]

In other words, thinking like a Christian is less important than looking like one and acting like one in a Christian environment. Christianity is more membership in a club than it is smart, intelligent membership in the world. This means that, to many Christians, their involvement in the world is a necessary evil at best. At worst it is fraternizing with the enemy. No wonder few Christians have a worldview that incorporates the world as it really is.

If the wider world is a Christian's enemy, then a Christian is certainly not going to think about finding God there. Such a Christian is thinking more about fighting the world and running skirmishes in and out of it than they are connecting with their world in any way. Seeking for God in the wider world is not an activity carried out by many Christians when it is believed that God is not to be found there in the first place. It's almost as if some have rewritten John 3:16 to read: "God so hated the world that he gave his only begotten Son, that whoever believes in him should not have to face the world any more, but shall have everlasting immunity from it."

This is where the Christian subculture has been detrimental to our witness and our worship in the world. The Christian thing is set over and against the world's thing, and rarely is it thought to be in and around it. Christian radio plays only Christian songs. Christian bookstores sell only Christian books. The implication of this is that all other books and all other songs are either dangerous or of no value to the Christian.

If Christians are to have any positive influence in the world, this model will have to change. In their book on the church adjusting to the new millennium, *Growing Spiritual Redwoods*, William M. Easum and Thomas G. Bandy picture the world as a forest in which the true Christian witness comes from spiritual redwoods—tall strong trees, rooted and growing right in the middle of the forest's density.

> The church has always been wary of the forest. Its deep shadows and sudden illuminations seemed to encourage all manner of talk about gods, goddesses, and demons. Fertility cults, competing

spiritualities, mystical experiences, and supernatural speculations surround authentic Christian faith. In the past, the church tended to attack the forest, chopping it down to make way for cathedrals of dogmatic or ideological correctness. Church leaders erected multiple gateways to guard the entrances to their denominationally homogeneous churches. Hurdles of baptism counseling, membership training, and institutional assimilation ensured that none of the mud of the forest ever made it into the "City of God." Yet as the structures and institutions of the twentieth century crumble, the forest infringes upon society once again.[3]

Christians who are ready for these changes will be ones who are rooted in the world as people of faith. They will be those who are finding and worshiping God in church and in the world as well. How will this be done? Through seeking a hidden God and believing that indeed, he can be found anywhere, all the time, where you least expect him.

This is not optional. If you want to follow God's work in the world and keep up with the movements of the Holy Spirit, you will have to start thinking like this. The next generation of Christians is not buying the Christian subculture. Many of them have been raised in it and are now finding its answers inadequate for the world they are inhabiting. Which is one of the reasons this discussion is so important, because if they do not find God in the wider world, they will run the risk of losing their faith altogether.

FOUR

The Cultural Christian and the Christian in Culture

We do not attack the inhabitants of the culture; we rescue them. We act shrewdly, not for self-protection, but to bring others into the kingdom.

TODD HAHN AND DAVID VERHAAGEN[1]

Meet Jack. He attends a Christian college, listens mostly to Christian music, grew up in a Christian home, and has always had Christians as his best friends. Jack is wary of the world, and because of that he is uncomfortable around non-Christians. When he witnesses, he usually witnesses to strangers—people he will probably never see again.

God is a big part of Jack's day without him even thinking about it. Attending chapel, singing worship songs, or reading his Bible for the required Bible course are routine. He prays sometimes at night before he goes to bed and feels a little guilty when he thinks about how long it's been since he last prayed, but then he remembers he prayed in chapel that day. That's a given, at least three days a week, not to mention the classes he has that start with devotions and prayer. When it comes right down to it, Jack really doesn't have to concern himself very much with being a Christian; a large amount of Christianity is already programmed into his day.

His parents love the fact that Jack is at a Christian college; that's why they are paying for it. They can rest assured about his training as a Christian as well as his protection from the world. Though they would never admit this, they also like the fact that the school will see to it that Jack looks and acts like a Christian whether he likes it or not.

When he first came to school at the Christian college, Jack was more into praying and Bible reading than he is now. He even attended a freshman Bible study on his floor, but he's kind of gotten away from that now that he's a senior and busy with sports and a steady girl. Jack rarely goes to movies, but his favorite TV show is *Friends*.

Jack will go on to marry his steady girl from college and become a computer programmer for a small software company near the town where he grew up. In this setting he will keep up his church attendance, but his Christianity pretty much will go underground outside of that. As was always the case for him, Jack's friends will continue to revolve around people he knows at church. Of course, he will have acquaintances at work, but he will have so little in common with them that he will rarely associate with them outside of the required work setting. As far as witnessing goes, he never did figure out how to witness to someone he sees every day, so he will pretty much stop witnessing altogether.

Part of this is because no one talked to him about witnessing as a part of his life. It was always a category on a spiritual checklist—nothing tied to real relationships, since he never really had any real relationships with non-Christians anyway. But the other reason is that his Christianity was always a cultural thing, and outside of a Christian subculture, it will hardly come up in his mind or conversations. His Christianity will be at odds with the world he lives in over half the time. In the end, he will live in two worlds, the Christian one and the secular one. He will remain a committed Christian, but that will only increase his frustration of having to move back and forth between worlds.

A Cultural Christian

Jack is typical of what I would call a cultural Christian. To the cultural Christian, the world is a scary place to be avoided at all costs. The products and services marketed and sold to cultural Christians help them do just that. They provide a safer alternative to the world, and as such they ensure cultural Christians can keep their distance from the world. Of course, this can't happen all the time—Christians have to live and work in the world—but it can happen enough to create two separate worlds that divide up a cultural Christian's life.

In order to survive in this environment, then, the cultural Christian has to have an invisible line down the center of everything, separating Christian from secular, good from evil. Cultural Christians tend to let other people define these lines for them, especially pastors and those in positions of authority. For instance, if their pastor says Harry Potter is dangerous for their kids, cultural Christians will adopt that point of view, and even add their voice to a campaign against Harry Potter books, when they have never read one personally. Cultural Christians seem to go along with the crowd. They tend to uncritically accept the popular Christian version of things, thus trusting the subculture to interpret the world to them and authorize for them that which is good and bad.

The more a person lives with these black and white definitions of things, the less relevant his faith becomes in the secular arena. He gets used to having someone else think for him. The secular world becomes something the cultural Christian has to somehow endure. It is assumed the Christian alternative will be taken wherever it applies. To not select the Christian option is to be worldly.

Jill

And then there's Jill. Let's put her in the same Christian college as Jack so we can see more sharply the differences in her and Jack's perspectives. Jill grew up in a Christian home as well, albeit a much more open one than Jack's. Her family moved often, so she never really got connected to a church youth group. She always went to public schools, and most of her friends, including best friends, were non-Christians. She tried the youth group, in fact she got baptized on one of their river raft trips, but she didn't last very long with the group because she never found her place there. So she continued with her non-Christian friends, whom she found more honest and more loyal than the Christian kids. Her lifestyle of partying with these friends would have raised eyebrows in the church, but in spite of appearances, her faith was working on her insides. Jill's faith affected her love for people, her enjoyment of God's world, and her passion for non-Christians. It didn't manifest itself in so much of the external things and Christian behavior that indicate a Christian life to a cultural Christian.

When it came time for college, Jill went away to a large university that offered the kind of courses she was after. There she lived in a house with three other girls and continued her life blending in with non-Christians, but by her junior year she had decided she wanted to try a more Christian environment and transferred to Jack's college, which is where she is now.

This has turned out to be a sort of mixed blessing for her. On one hand, the Christian teaching and perspective has been good for her soul, but she still has a terrible time belonging anywhere. Though her faith is growing, she has not had the same homogeneous background as most of the students who have been Christian-schooled most of their lives. To her, this whole school is like a glorified youth group—more like Christian camp than college. To the other students, she seems worldly and forward. To Jill, they seem superficial and after nothing other than a Christian mate. The few friends she does make end up being underclassmen, drawn to her because they feel they can trust her. She ends up being an unwitting counselor because these younger students feel freer talking to Jill about their struggles than they do the resident assistant.

To Jill, the students at this college have a Christian life mediated by a Christian environment that deals almost exclusively with externals. Jill finds this environment stifling to her faith. She recently told her parents, "I loved God more before I came here." As a result, she will transfer back to the university for her final year and go on to a career in medical technology. She will marry much later in life than most of the girls at the Christian college because she wants to experience traveling and pushing her limit in extreme sports.

Jill's faith is going to grow more after college until it takes up a very big part of her life. All along, however, she will continue her life among non-Christians because she loves them and sees them as created in God's image and important to him. Jill will find that her love for God is not in conflict with her love for the world. She will find them actually one and the same because she finds God wherever she goes. What one might call her "witnessing" will hardly look like anything Jack might recognize as witnessing. It will come out of her love for people and the natural sharing of her life with them. Unlike Jack, strangers would be the last people Jill would ever witness to.

A Christian in Culture

Jill is what I would call a Christian in culture. Christians in culture are different from cultural Christians in that they have not been acculturated in the Christian subculture, or if they have, they have found a way out. To the Christian in culture, the world is an exciting place, full of God's presence and good things he has made. Everywhere they go, they find that God got there first. (Cultural Christians have the audacity to think that they are actually bringing God to the world along with them—that he's not there until they get there.)

A cultural Christian is defined by Christian things and Christian behaviors. Their Christianity is more like an adjective. The Christian things around them make them Christian. A Christian in culture is more like a noun. A Christian in culture is a Christian regardless of where you put them or with whom. Their Christianity has more to do with their thinking and less with behavior and identification. To quote Colleen McDannell again from the last chapter, "The stress that is placed on critically thinking about religion in liberal traditions holds less importance [to cultural Christians] than doing religious activities and identifying oneself as Christian." The cultural Christian doesn't have to think much about their Christianity because they are in the presence of Christians and surrounded by Christian things.

When the cultural Christian is outside the Christian subculture, they are like fish out of water. They usually resort to one of two behaviors: they either wear their Christianity like a badge and constantly try to "evangelize" the non-Christians around them, or they retreat into a shell, shun most relationships except those necessary to carrying on business in the world, and hardly ever bring their faith out at all.

By contrast, the Christian in culture sees their Christianity as a function of who they are, not what they buy, wear, or listen to. Their faith is not even a function of who they are with, because they can be with anybody and not compromise or hide what they believe. It's just that they don't have to parade what they believe, either. They know that this world belongs to God and that all truth comes from him, so there will be many opportunities to bring up their faith should they feel it is time to do so.

A Christian in culture sees God everywhere, wherever they look and wherever they are. They have an inner vision of God that directs their perception and understanding of things. The cultural Christian, on the other hand, is more apt to deal in externals, and thus it is important for them to know that things are clearly Christian by way of some sort of identification. One can easily see the importance of a Christian industry marketing Christian products and services to Christian people.

Two Christians

In an earlier book I introduced my readers to a person I called Anna of Middleton, because she was from Middleton,

Massachusetts, and I never got her last name. I met her at a Christian rock festival in New England, and what set her apart was her age (she was in her seventies), and the fact that she was thoroughly enjoying the faith expressed by the young Christians at this event who were singing and playing a style of music she had no business understanding. No matter; she got the message from their heart to hers without having it go through her head. At the same event was a middle-aged man in a wheelchair who was bitterly complaining about the very same event. When I encountered him, he had cornered one of the singers and was verbally abusing her for not mentioning Jesus enough in her song lyrics.

These two people are typical of the two different types of Christians being discussed. The man in the wheelchair needed to hear Jesus named over and over again to satisfy himself that this event was indeed a Christian event and that it was glorifying to God. Anna, on the other hand, seemed to find Jesus everywhere, whether he was mentioned or not, and as far as I could tell, she was in a continual state of glorifying God. Her worship came from within her. Worship for the man, as is so often the case with cultural Christians, had to be a clearly defined event. It had to come from somewhere outside himself in order to bring him into a spirit of worship. When that didn't happen to his satisfaction, his expectations of this concert as a Christian event were not met.

Safe for the Whole Family

To the cultural Christian, the world is a very scary place, to be avoided whenever possible. Because of this and as evidence of a predominant fear of the world, safety has emerged as one of the central issues for cultural Christians, and one of the main reasons a cultural Christianity exists. This safety is ensured by keeping one's distance from the world when at all possible, and Christian schools, radio, music, and television help keep that cultural distance.

A local programmer for Christian radio recently reported to me that a listener called in irate over the fact that her seven-year-old had to be subjected to offensive murders and slashings on a news report on his station. This happened to also be during the DC sniper scare when the message from the perpetrator was going out, "Your kids are not safe. Your kids are not safe." The woman's comment was telling: "Don't you people screen the news before you air it?" According to the programmer, the news is on a live feed. Screening is impossible. This is typical of the world a cultural Christian wants to live in—a world where what is violent and offensive, even in the news, is shielded from the ears of the Christian. The programmer is in a dilemma, because the radio station has advertised itself as "Safe for the whole family." In this case, what the station promised, it cannot deliver, because hardly any news about the world is safe anymore. And so the cultural Christian is wary of the world, suspicious, afraid, and defensive toward all who do not share the same beliefs.

On the other hand, and in spite of its real danger, Christians in culture realize the dangers of being in the world, but they also know that Jesus prayed for their protection and is now at the right hand of God the Father to ensure it (John 17:15). Christians in culture are secure in Christ. They know that truth is right up next to falsehood and that evil is mixed in with good, but they also know they have been given the Holy Spirit and a mandate to uncover the good in the world (1 Timothy 4:4). They have the Word of God to help them set apart truth (John 17:17). And they have their senses trained to distinguish good from evil (Hebrews 5:14). In other words, living in the world for the Christian in culture is not a walk in the park, but neither is it an impossibility or a hindrance to faith. It is a challenge to be met with courage and the anticipation that those who seek God in all things will truly find him. Thus, a Christian in culture can be hope-filled, trusting, and positively engaged with the world around them.

Harry Potter and Archaeology

An example of these two approaches to the world can be graphically illustrated in the different way in which Christians reacted to the overwhelming popularity of the Harry Potter books among children in recent years. These stories by J.K. Rowling are about a young English boy who enters a fantasy world of witches, warlords, and magic. In many ways they are not unlike C.S. Lewis' Chronicles of Narnia, where ordinary British children turn out to be kings and queens in another land where they team up with talking animals and fight witches and other creatures with supernatural powers for good and for evil. The problem with the Harry Potter stories is that the hero comes from a line of human witches and is himself in training to perfect the use of his own wizardry.

Although the author is herself a professed Christian (a member of the Anglican church), and her stories are full of the struggle of good and evil (Harry is fighting hard to stay on the side of the good), because she has chosen to place her stories in a world of witches, potions, spells, and incantations, her books have created understandable controversy among Christians and even more so because of their popularity.

The initial reaction to these books in the Christian subculture was swift and final. Nothing good could possibly come out of stories for children that glorified witchcraft. Even if they are "harmless" fantasies, they may lead Christian kids to get interested in real witches as a result. Very soon after this became an issue in the subculture there was an immediate groundswell of widespread panic.

Opinions travel fast when fear and suspicion rule. All it takes are a few influential people in church to raise the warning flag and suddenly everyone is an expert on what is wrong. Unfortunately, the opinions that fly around during these skirmishes are largely uninformed and mostly emotional in content. Few who press the panic button have even looked at the real issues or discussed their ramifications. Almost none have actually read even one of the books they are condemning; they take someone else's word for it. A cultural Christian's bias is already firmly entrenched against culture. This just focuses the angst on one thing. Finally they have the culprit. Here's something they can actually do something about. Cultural Christians love to be against things in the wider world—something they perceive they can stop. Anti-cultural movements like this give the enemy a face. "They're after our kids, and we're not going to let them get us this time."

A Christian in culture looks at something like this very differently. The first thing to do is to become better informed. What are these books actually like? Who is the author? Why are they popular? Is there a real danger? If so, what exactly is it? If we are going to engage our culture, shouldn't we have something more intelligent to bring to the discussion than a knee-jerk emotional reaction? In this case, the answers to these questions begin to change the picture quite a bit from the widespread panic of the cultural Christian.

A Christian in culture tends to be looking for the good first. The bad is assumed to be there due to the fall, but why focus on it (Proverbs 11:27)? Good can also be found, so why not find that? Something undeniable about these books is their universal appeal. They are so popular among young readers that kids will line up for hours at bookstores waiting for the release of a new story. In an age of visual assault from computers, television, and film, anything that would capture the imagination of children should at least be looked at more carefully. If anything, these stories are getting kids reading, and that part is good.

A more thorough look at these stories finds a typical struggle between good and evil that is common to all good literature. It is the presence of witchcraft on both sides of this battle that creates a problem for Christians. And yet, these stories take place in an imaginary world. They are not about calling up evil powers to effect events in the real world. Children old enough to understand this can enjoy these stories without being led into Satanism or the occult. One commentator on these books has humorously postulated that Harry Potter is to real witchcraft what Fred Flintstone is to archaeology.

Christians in culture look at phenomena like this as an opportunity to join in the discussion as Christians in the world instead of the Christian-against-the-world reaction common to cultural Christians. If these stories have made a connection with the general public, is there any way we can use this for the good? Christian author Connie Neal has done this very thing. In her book *The Gospel According to Harry Potter* (Westminster John Knox Press), she has turned the table on these discussions. Not only is she helping Christians to interpret these books, she is using their popularity among non-Christians as an opportunity to get them to look into the gospel. She has found what she calls "glimmers of the gospel" in these stories—enough that she can tell the gospel story to people who may have never heard it but are familiar with the Harry Potter stories.

Many Christians have closed the book on Harry Potter. "On the flip side," said Neal in an interview for *The Repository* in Canton, Ohio, "many people have closed the book on Christians, and they probably have never read the gospel...I hope and pray that you will actually see the gospel in a way you've never seen it before."[2]

The article goes on to say that she believes Christians should actively engage popular culture. "I'm a Christian who wants to be a light shining in the darkness."[3] A good example of a Christian in culture.

These two types of Christians—cultural Christians and Christians in culture—are admittedly gross generalizations. People rarely fit completely into any of the categories described in this chapter, but discussions like this do help to identify ways of thinking by magnifying the differences. This book is seeking to develop the thought processes of a Christian in culture, and this chapter will help put that kind of

Christian and that kind of thinking into context with what may also be common among Christians. We will turn now to look at how these two types of approaches to culture have radically different worldviews.

FIVE

All Truth Is God's Truth

I've seen fire and I've seen rain.

JAMES TAYLOR

❖ ❖ ❖

I was on the road October 20, 2001, when a number of rock, pop, and movie stars gathered in New York's Madison Square Garden to entertain an audience of 6000 firefighters, police officers, emergency workers, and their families and thank them for their dedication and hard work in the aftermath of the September 11 tragedy. I had an appearance to attend to that night, so I was only able to see the beginning of the show, yet when I returned almost four hours later, I was surprised to see it still running. In all this concert had over six hours of viewing time.

At the end of the show they flashed up scenes of earlier participants, and I found that James Taylor was there and he had sung one of his classics from the 1970s, "Fire and Rain." Because I knew that song, as I did a lot of his early music, I got out my guitar and sang it again for my own benefit. I was not prepared for the emotional experience I encountered. I could barely make it through the song, even by myself, and could only imagine what it must have meant to the audience that night.

The actual meaning behind the opening lines of "Fire and Rain" have remained obscure to most of Taylor's followers over

the last 30 years. We all assumed this song was about something deeply personal—a painful loss he had to capture in a
song in order to cope. He talks about losing a close friend
named Suzanne and how someone's plans had spelled her
mysterious end. He then captured his emotional disorienta-
tion by writing down the words of a song he can't remember
what to do with.

But in this new setting that night in New York, a chilling
prophetic accuracy came over this song. Suddenly Suzanne
was just one in over 3000 who died that unforgettable day, and
it was the plans of a few terrorists that brought an end to her—
and them—leaving a nation disoriented and distraught. Like
James, we wrote down our feelings, but we didn't know what
to do with them.

What else but fire and rain could adequately express the
fiery debris that rained down on Manhattan that day—a sunny
day we all thought would never end? And what about the
loneliness all those workers experienced in the first few hours
and days after the attack, digging through rubble, trying to
find friends they always thought they would see again?

The uncanny accuracy of this song for such a moment was
reminiscent of the prophetic books of the Bible, which carry a
two-pronged fulfillment of their prophecies. Many of these
prophecies had a particular application to an immediate situation as well as a long-term fulfillment centuries later (some are
yet to be fulfilled), captured in words that meant entirely
different things in each setting. A classic example would be
David's prayer in Psalm 22 that contained graphic descrip-
tions of death by crucifixion—unknown in David's time—and
yet had other implications to David when he wrote it. Jesus
quoted from this psalm in his last words from the cross. In
other words, David wrote a song about his own oppressed
state and unknowingly provided Jesus with the words he
would later cry from the cross—words like: "My God, why
have you forsaken me?" (See Psalm 22:1; Matthew 27:46.)

This same phenomenon was chillingly obvious in the
second verse of Taylor's song when he lamented the demise of

his first rock group, the Flying Machines, and unknowingly detailed the means by which the World Trade Center would be brought down. In the song he has the Flying Machines broken up in pieces all over the ground. And now, of course, we all know the damage wrought by four flying machines on that fateful day in 2001.

I'm not suggesting that James Taylor was writing Scripture, but I would entertain the possibility that God could have inspired these words because he had a particular message he wanted to deliver to people in the aftermath of the tragedy, so he planted this song in the conscience of a generation that it might touch them in a time like this and turn their thoughts towards the Savior.

I say this because the last verse contains a prayer where James Taylor cries out for help in coping with his loss. This last verse has always been a mystery to me, because Taylor has never made any public statement of faith, and yet this verse is a prayer, not even to a general God, but to Jesus by name. In it he claims that he cannot make it any further in life unless he gets divine help from Jesus himself.

No one could have come up with a better prayer for that moment and time than this. And no one, other than a nationally known celebrity, could have had access to this particular platform to deliver it. But that need not hinder the Holy Spirit. Could it not be that James Taylor, like David, wrote a song about his own oppressed state that, 30 years later, provided words that God could use to comfort thousands (and millions through television and video)—even calling upon the name and person of Jesus Christ as the source of that comfort? Whether or not you see this as the possible work of God depends a lot on your worldview.

A Riddle

What is it that everyone has but most people don't know what it is? We rarely ever talk about it, and yet it controls many of the everyday decisions we make in life. You may not even know you have one, but you won't let go of yours. Most people in the same group have the same one. It's not taught as much as it is caught. And because it is ingrained over a lifetime of learning, it is hard—though not impossible—to change. What is it? It's your worldview—the way you see the world, and specific to this discussion, the way God fits (or doesn't fit) into your picture of the world.

For instance, one particular Christian worldview would reject the idea of God speaking prophetically through a secular pop song sung by a person who is at least not known to be a Christian. This position, most commonly held by cultural Christians, holds to the point of view that God's activity in the world is largely confined to Christians. In this worldview, an invisible curtain separates Christian things from secular, worldly things. The Christian things are determined by their source and their labels. Christian songs, for instance, are obviously Christian because they are created by Christian artists, marketed by a Christian industry, and sold in Christian bookstores. They are also songs full of clear Christian messages. Like the man in the wheelchair in the last chapter, a Christian who holds to this view becomes upset when a Christian song is ambiguous and doesn't have a clearly identifiable Christian message. That seems pointless and should not be allowed. "What do we have Christian music for anyway? If you want songs about worldly things, go to the world for that." This statement makes perfect sense to many cultural Christians who hold this worldview.

Consequently, anything that didn't come through this Christian "pipeline" is secular and suspect by default. God is personally involved with what happens on only one side of the curtain. Satan rules the other side, and there is a continual culture war going on between these two sides. God could not possibly be at work on the other side of the curtain. As nice as it was for all those rock stars and movie stars to put on that event in New York, they still are non-Christians with immoral lifestyles and comedians with foul language and dirty jokes. Most are probably abortion advocates, and some of them are openly gay. God was certainly not present in this event. It was on the wrong side of the curtain. One worldview demands this conclusion.

Another worldview might not have any problem with finding God active in this way in the world. This worldview, more in line with that of a Christian in culture, celebrates God as Creator and Lord over all creation. Though the creation has fallen, it still can reflect the goodness he put into it in the beginning. (Think of nature that bears the mark of the fall [Romans 8:20-21] and yet is also capable of breathtaking beauty.) All life and breath has value and can receive common grace from a God who is in love with what he made. We know that because of his justice, sin must be punished and the wages of sin is death (Romans 6:23), but those wages are not all paid until the end, and God will not get any pleasure out of this, by the way. Scripture even tells us it is not his desire for any to perish, but for everyone to come to repentance (2 Peter 3:9). He has provided a sacrifice for sin and wishes that all would receive it. In the meantime, God is withholding his wrath against everyone (2 Peter 3:7), allowing a level of love and happiness to be shared in this life by even those who do not claim Christ as Savior.

The universe is built on the laws of God. Those who don't necessarily believe in God can discover these laws and reap the benefits of respecting them. In this way, they may partake of God without knowing it or giving him credit or praise. The Christian does know this, however, so it is possible to give God praise for that which an unbeliever is unconscious of or even taking personal credit for. I'm thinking of an athlete who excels in the use of natural talent. The athlete may develop a big head over his incredible performances—he may even insult God—but that need not stop a Christian from praising God for the power and beauty of the human body as expressed by the athlete and marvel at what it is capable of. This is the worldview I adhere to and recommend as a worldview that will serve a Christian well. It will travel well with a Christian into culture and allow him or her to find

God active on both sides of the imaginary line dividing the Christian and the secular. Indeed, it erases the line altogether.

Because it is not God's desire for any to perish, when over 3000 die in one savage act, and the survivors gather together in one building, God is there, and I believe his sorrow greatly outdistances the sorrow of them all combined. James Taylor may have sung the song, but God was in the words, calling people to seek comfort in Jesus. If in seeking God I find him in the song of James Taylor and the ministry of that song in what some would call a "secular" setting, then I am privileged to own that point of view and praise God for what I believe he has done.

Two Views

It's important to note that a worldview is not truth; it is the grid through which one perceives the world. You could say it is a way of arranging the world in one's mind. Everyone's worldview is slightly different. It is made up of how we were raised, where we were raised, who we have exposed ourselves and our thinking to, and how much we have sought to think for ourselves about what we believe. People who don't think for themselves very much, especially when it comes to spiritual things, have more homogeneous worldviews, because they, by and large, adopt the worldview of the larger group. People who think for themselves have more varying worldviews, even differing in some aspects with the group they happen to travel in. Worldviews are adjustable—some, more easily than others. A good worldview, then, is one by which truth can be more accurately observed. A bad worldview would make it harder to find truth, like a bad pair of glasses might distort one's vision of everything.

The two general worldviews discussed so far show two radically different ways of relating to the world. In one, the Christian is the antagonist; in the other, the Christian is a synthesist. One stands in opposition to the world; the other operates within and alongside it. One is at war with the world, the other is at peace, looking for what can be affirmed. One runs from and rejects the world, the other runs into it and makes contributions. One seeks evil it can fight, the other seeks good it can embrace. One emphasizes the fall, the other emphasizes creation. In one, the Christian is defensive; in the other, the Christian is open-minded. In one, the world is "out to get us"; in the other, the world is merely "being what it is." One puts truth outside culture, the other finds truth in culture. One categorically rejects the world, the other selectively accepts it.

One worldview cites "Do not love the world or anything in the world" (1 John 2:15). The other finds "Seek the peace and prosperity of the city to which I have carried you into exile. Pray to the LORD for it, because if it prospers, you too will prosper" (Jeremiah 29:7 NIV). And "make every effort to live in peace with everyone" (Hebrews 12:14). This is the worldview of a Christian in culture.

Making an Impact

Worldviews can also make a huge difference in how we approach making an impact in the world.

Imagine walking into a bookstore full of intelligent, high-quality Christian books as well as intelligent, high-quality non-Christian books. The store is owned and operated by Christians and most of the salespeople are Christians as well. Their purpose is to help guide you to the books you want, be they Christian or otherwise. Instead of Joybells Christian Bookstore, this store might be named Quality Books. People who aren't Christians will go to this bookstore because they like the environment and they can find what they are looking for. In the process they may very well be introduced to books by excellent Christian writers they otherwise would never discover.

Or how about this: a movie which in essence assumes the possibility that human beings were created in the image of a loving Creator. It would not necessarily be about the gospel or someone being converted to Christianity. It would not be recognized as a "Christian" movie, although it would come from the perspective of a Christian worldview. This would be a standard Hollywood movie (or an enterprising independent film that was gaining attention by its excellent quality), not a Christian takeover of the industry by buying theater time and recruiting Christians from churches to storm the evil "denizens of the deep." Christians might be behind the funding and creating of this movie, but no one would know it. It would not be a movie whose purpose was to provide wholesome entertainment for Christians. It might not even be "wholesome." It might be rated "R." It might have to be, to make in impact on this culture.

How you view this would depend a lot on your worldview. These two types of approaches would be seen by the antagonist as selling out to the world and watering down the message. But to the synthesist, they would be small but significant ways of making an impact in the world by engaging culture, introducing a Christian point of view into the mainstream market, and being salt and light in the movie industry.

A World of Difference

In the movie *K-19: The Widowmaker,* Harrison Ford plays a crusty Russian captain who is put in charge of a hastily completed nuclear submarine in the early 1960s during the height of the Cold War. As the new captain, he is put in the difficult position of having to usurp the authority of the original captain (played by Liam Neeson) without divulging the details and reasons for his secret mission from the Kremlin. As can be expected, a power struggle ensues during most of their voyage, which dances with danger of nuclear global consequence. Though Neeson's character disagrees with the new captain's orders, he reluctantly complies out of respect for the chain of command.

Thinking he is doing a favor for his former captain and crew, a loyal lieutenant seizes the opportunity to pull a gun on Harrison Ford and locks him up. When the former captain (Neeson) finds out about this, instead of praising the lieutenant's actions, he puts him under arrest and frees Ford to continue running the ship. This move of support dramatically changes the situation on the sub. The new captain no longer is the lone man in charge, fighting everyone on board as well as his own conscience over the difficult decisions he must make. Now he is free to make better decisions for the right reasons and the good of everyone on board.

Sometimes we make wrong decisions out of mere antagonism and frustration at the evil world we live in. We fight everyone and everything that does not hold to a Christian belief. We see all non-Christians as our enemies. Seeing everything as covered by a blanket of evil can cloud our vision of what God might be doing in and through culture. I believe this is what is meant by the proverb "He who seeks good finds goodwill, but evil comes to him who searches for it" (Proverbs 11:27). If we are fighting the evil in the world all the time, we can easily miss the good. We can even lock up the wrong enemy sometimes. A worldview can make a world of difference.

Jesus in the Headlines

Our pastor will periodically preach a sermon based on something off the front page of the *Los Angeles Times* from the previous Wednesday. What makes this unique is that he tells us about this ahead of time. He'll do it for two or three weeks in a row. Because I am an avid newspaper reader, I will e-mail him my suggestions as soon as I get Wednesday's paper, just for the fun of it. Now it would be one thing to get up on a Sunday and relate the sermon to something that was newsworthy that week, but to announce ahead of time that there will be something worth a sermon on the front page of one newspaper on a given day that particular week says something about our pastor's worldview. He's not hoping there will be something spiritual on the front page of the newspaper on Wednesday; he is modeling for his congregation that there is a spiritual way of looking at the front page on any day. He could do this for every article, every day, if he wanted. And we can do it too.

Recently there was, in fact, something about God in the newspaper, and it turned out be a disaster. A recent column in the *Los Angeles Times* was titled "Jesus in a Geo? It Would Be a Miracle." It was about a Pennsylvania-based evangelical environmental organization that was running a "What Would Jesus Drive?" campaign against gas-guzzling sports utility vehicles. The head of the organization argued that "God would choose an environmentally friendly vehicle, such as a Toyota Prius, which has a hybrid gasoline-electric motor."[1] The heading on the continuation of the article page read: "Pastor puts Jesus behind the wheel."

Immediately next to the Jesus-in-a-Geo article is a picture of a Japanese violin prodigy known simply as Midori addressing a room full of students at the Music Academy of Hamilton High in Los Angeles. The article reports her telling kids the truth about practice time, hard work, concentration, and the universal appeal of music. Her visit to the school was part of a two-week "On Location" residency with the Los Angeles Philharmonic.

"I believe that music is something that we should be able to take for granted," she said. "It's one of the ways that make each one of us individual and also makes us have an identity as human apart from other living beings, to have the arts as a conscious form of expression." [2]

Midori, a celebrated violinist who debuted with Zubin Mehta and the New York Philharmonic at age 11, has created a foundation that has reached more than 100,000 students in New York City public schools with free music education.

Though the silly Jesus-as-an-environmentalist article mentions God and Jesus numerous times and quotes a Christian leader, I found God all over the Midori article that actually never referred to him at all. The contrast of these articles side by side was telling. One was embarrassing to my faith, the other was full of the truth of God's gifts to his creation and a marvelous example of using them well. Because all truth is God's truth, the article that never mentioned God was actually all about him, while the article that was all about Jesus, including a picture of him praying over a freeway, wasn't about God at all. It came from a cultural Christianity and would be heralded in some circles of the Christian subculture as a major blow for the kingdom, when, in fact, any thinking Christian in culture would recognize it as untrue, if not a dubious, even blasphemous, characterization of the Godhead.

Finding God in the world is more a factor of our looking for truth than it is a victory for getting Jesus in the headlines. And those who look diligently will be rewarded handsomely by finding him everywhere. What Midori found out about music was not much different than what young David found out playing his harp for King Saul, and at probably about the same age Midori began her career. From reading that article, I thanked God that morning for his good gifts and learned something I could apply to using my own.

The implication of this is much more far reaching than the newspaper. In fact, apart from some outright sin or anti-Christian endeavor, it's hard to imagine anything not having some good in it that can be celebrated by the believer as something worthy of praise.

In order to appreciate and enjoy a sacred life, then, we need to search for what is Christian about everything we do. Things don't become Christian by being called Christian. They become Christian when they are transformed in our minds to conform to God's will. "Do not conform to the pattern of this world," writes Paul in Romans 12:2, "but be transformed by the renewing of your mind." The renewing of our minds will transform our experience. "Then you will be able to test and approve [or live out] what God's will is." All of this, he calls our "spiritual act of worship" (Romans 12:1 NIV). This is not a Sunday morning worship service;

this goes on all the time, as in any Wednesday morning. This is a life of worship—a life lived continually seeking and continually finding.

When to Fight and When to Embrace

I conclude this chapter with some thoughts from Chap Clark, Ph.D., of Fuller Seminary, in an Internet article, "A Hierarchy of Theological Responses to Popular Culture: Knowing When to Fight, Knowing When to Embrace." His is an inspiring challenge both to find truth and contribute to its furtherance in the world.

> God is constantly in the business of revealing his love and purposes to those he loves. That God would care to use the medium of popular art, narrative and culture to teach us all something about ourselves, believers and non-believers alike, lines up with his heart and his character of pursuing love as revealed in the Parable of the Good Shepherd (Luke 15)....
>
> Perhaps it is time for believers to first acknowledge that we are all part of the culture in which we live, and God has placed us there to be light and salt to those we live amongst. Maybe the day has come that no longer is the church something a person goes to when she is ready to "seek," but experiences when she sits at a coffee shop with a Christ-following friend with whom she has cried during a moving film. Could it be that God is calling us all—believers and non-believers alike—to allow ourselves to hear God's whisper through a song, or a book, or even a beer commercial and that as his ambassadors it is our calling to point others to the source of the Truth that stirred within the human soul?

May we all recognize that God does indeed speak in and through culture, in ways our theological categories rarely allow us to see, and that we can join with the Apostle Paul in helping people to see God in the everyday of human activity, art and culture as he says, "Finally, brothers, whatever is true, whatever is noble, whatever is right, whatever is pure, whatever is lovely, whatever is admirable—if anything is excellent or praiseworthy—think about such things" (Philippians 4:8).[3]

This statement, "If anything is excellent or praiseworthy" indicates that Paul is talking about a discerning process of finding truth in the world. He can't be talking about focusing only on biblical truth, in which case there would be no question as to the presence of that which is excellent and praiseworthy. You would only say "if there is something excellent and praiseworthy" about something that had the potential of being devoid of these things. He is clearly speaking about what we encounter daily in the world where there is a question as to the validity of things. At the same time, his admonition to find these things in the world, is, in itself, an affirmation that there will be something valuable to find. We will look at this verse again in a later chapter, but it is important at this point to note this as Paul's verification of the discerning process of finding truth outside of its expected places.

I can still hear the voice of Dr. Arthur Holmes, then chair of the department of philosophy at Wheaton College, ringing down the halls of my alumni memories: "All truth is God's truth." Truth, whether it's in a Spielberg film, a John Irving novel, a stunning sunset, or a James Taylor song, always leads me back to its source. And since I am in love with its source, I can worship God anew upon the discovery of each new thing.

SIX

What's Good About It?

*When we're all caught up in all the things we're against,
we forget the beauty of the things we're supposed to
be for. We forget what the kingdom of God
looks like and all the wonderfully odd
characters taking up residence there."*[1]

DAVID DARK

The LORD God made garments of skin for Adam
and his wife and clothed them. And the LORD
God said, "The man has now become like one of
us, knowing good and evil. He must not be
allowed to reach out his hand and take also from
the tree of life and eat, and live forever." So the
LORD God banished him from the Garden of Eden
to work the ground from which he had been
taken (Genesis 3:21-23).

When Adam and Eve were bumped from the garden, it
was a good thing. They had become too much like God
for their own fig leaves. Knowing good and evil is one thing;
always doing the right thing with that knowledge is something
else. Unable to choose good all the time, or to not let evil creep
into the good and infect it from the inside, our ancestors had
to be removed from the garden lest they or their offspring
"take also from the tree of life and eat, and live forever."
Eating of the tree of life after having disobeyed God would
have locked us forever in our disobedience, rebellion, and

77

weakness toward evil with no possibility of salvation. He banished us from the garden for our own good, so he could save us from sin and death and finally usher us into his paradise to partake of the tree of life and live forever as a redeemed race without threat of succumbing to evil's forces.

So here we are, living and breathing on this planet in a kind of suspended animation. The Lord told Adam and Eve they would die if they ate the forbidden fruit. Well, they ate and they died…not right away, mind you, but they died nonetheless. They are quite dead now—buried somewhere in the Fertile Crescent…gone to dust, but not forgotten.

So, thanks to them, death is on everyone's agenda. What is this thing we call life, then? It is a relatively short period of time we dance and languish on this planet. Few of us would want to live forever unless things significantly changed anyway. Some would rather die and get it over with. Though it has its moments, our current experience of life on earth is a very low-rent version of what God had in mind for us. And yet it is "life," and it's the only life we have known so far. It is conception, and birth, and a God-willing 70-year stint in a human body that peaks way too soon and unmercifully marches graveward with time, but it is also visited periodically by love, laughter, and joys that are accessible to all, regardless of one's eternal destination.

From a gospel standpoint, you could make a strong case for our one reason for breathing being to get right with God and secure our place with him in eternity. But what if that never happens? What if a person lives out Frank Sinatra's theme song, "I Did It My Way," and faces death and whatever it brings, head held high? What about that? Was it a waste? Was there no joy or beauty along the way? Was there no love given or received? Nothing to admire? Was there no point?

There is a point to this life short of regeneration. Solomon made this clear in Ecclesiastes, an Old Testament book which decries the meaninglessness of human existence "under the sun" (from a totally human perspective) and yet also acknowledges basic joys and satisfactions along the way.

God apparently allows for this. "Then I realized that it is good for a man to eat and drink, and find satisfaction in his toilsome labor under the sun during the few days of life God has given him—for this is his lot" (Ecclesiastes 5:18). This sentiment is repeated numerous times by the writer with slightly different wording but the same message: There are joys to be had in this brief life we live "under the sun," and the implication is that these are enjoyed by everyone, regardless of one's relationship with God.

One need not think too hard to see how such an understanding of creation and the fall can contribute much to our faith now outside the garden. If good can be gleaned from fallen humanity even this side of salvation and heaven, then Christians can find something to celebrate as truth in the world. People still aspire to the good even though evil is present. The knowledge given was of good as much as it was of evil. The origins of the dramatic arts, from Greek tragedies to Shakespeare, bear this out. They are, mostly all, morality plays that explore the war of good and evil within a person's soul. And don't we always want the good guy to win? Just because we are not capable of choosing good every time doesn't mean we can't still aspire to it.

Why Christians Like to Rain on the World's Parade

Thinking along these lines, however, poses some difficulties for many Christians. Evangelicals have never been very good at acknowledging that fallen humanity is capable of good or of enjoying life without grossly violating numerous laws of God. We are so committed to getting people saved that we often magnify the despicable nature of their unsaved state. We have a need to paint the unsaved in the worst possible light. But what if they happen to like their lives? What if they don't want to be saved? How can we justify Christianity when folks are already doing comparatively well?

Arguing along these lines—something Christians often do—leads to an unfortunate misrepresentation of the truth, because God is a good God who allows a measure of arbitrary grace to be granted to the human race. "He [God] causes his sun to rise on the evil and the good, and sends rain on the righteous and the unrighteous" (Matthew 5:45). Theologians often call this common grace. It is a grace Christians can celebrate just as we celebrate salvation, but this is a celebration rarely entered into by believers for many reasons, not the least of these being the sacred/secular worldview discussed in the last chapter that leaves God out of the minds of many Christians when they encounter the world. It makes it much simpler if the world is full of bad guys doing bad things.

We Christians always seem to want to rain on the world's parade. If non-Christians are actually enjoying life, then we think our theology is losing. It's not; it's just our bad theology. It's been true of legalistic Christianity as long as we have had it. In order for legalistic Christianity to work, we need worldly people to be miserable and decadent to justify our legalistic ban on eating, drinking, and being merry. If we can't have any fun, we have to find something wrong with everyone else's fun to justify our stringency.

I recently spent some time in an area of Indiana with a high Amish population and observed this attitude in its extreme forms. Both separation and legalism play heavily in the philosophy of this sect. The images are memorable. Black horse-drawn buggies were navigating two-way state and federal highways, necessitating some dangerous passing against oncoming traffic. Each buggy had a red triangle on the back for safety's sake, making it appear like a huge black widow spider from a distance, its tall thin wheels moving like spindly legs against a gray winter sky. As I passed them by, bearded men and bonneted women would stare grim-faced from inside their dark carriages. I looking at them, they looking at me...the two of us next to each other in two completely different worlds. I remember observing with no small level of irony that their horses were quite spirited. Lively horses, dour people. If I had to be in their world, I would want to be a horse. I felt decadent and worldly flying by them in my gas-guzzling, environment-altering automobile. I wonder sometimes if we appear to the world like the Amish did to me.

Actually, the whole Christian witnessing strategy once hinged on the argument that non-Christians are sinners living degenerate lives and experiencing the consequences of sin while Christians are getting it right even if we might not be so happy all the time. And as of late we have tried to throw off this unhappy part and prove that Christians have more fun. This is one of the unspoken tenets of contemporary Christianity, in fact, that the Christian life is better than its secular counterpart. In truth, we have the same conflicts and experience the same consequences as non-Christians. Christians are not exempt from the wages of sin. True, we have received forgiveness, but God cannot mock himself by excusing us from his own words. We all reap what we sow (Galatians 6:7).

Do Christians have more fun? I'm not sure it is even the point, especially in America, a country in which Christians constantly interpret blessing in terms contrary to what the Bible honors. The gospel needs better legs to stand on than this. Trying to sell Christianity by promising a better life with lots of unhappy Christians around can be interpreted as a farce by many. I believe it is a better witness to embrace that which is both good and bad about our human experience. Until Christians are real people, caught in the joys and sorrows of the human experience, but touched by the reality of the presence of God in their lives, the world is going to continue to get the wrong idea about following Christ, and we are going to continue to give them the wrong reasons for being saved. We are not saved to live a better life. We are saved to know God and enjoy him forever.

We need to reclaim that which is good about being human. A good deal of art—popular and classical—celebrates this. In doing so it is simply agreeing with the Creator when he created us and the world around us and pronounced it "good." These are things we can celebrate as Christians. We can even use our own appreciation of these things as a means of connecting with those who do not know God or acknowledge him as the source of good in their lives. If we share the sin and the resulting consequences, why not share the celebration of that which is good about the human experience? If we can connect, humanly speaking, with a preconverted world, that same world will be more apt to listen to us when we talk of God's grace and plan for salvation.

Got to Serve Somebody

Growing up in a fundamentalist environment that stressed "the fall of man," I always pegged the forbidden tree in the garden as a bad tree whose fruit brought evil into the world. Had the man and woman not eaten of it, they would have remained good. In truth, the tree made them more intelligent. The serpent was right. Their eyes were opened to both evil and good. Their newfound knowledge of evil made them aware of their own nakedness and how they could exploit it, and their newfound knowledge of good made them feel real guilt about this and a new need to hide and cover themselves.

The serpent actually deceived them with the truth. Everything he said would happen came true: "Your eyes will be opened, and you will be like God, knowing good and evil" (Genesis 3:5). Even God acknowledged that the man he created had become like him (Genesis 3:22). The lie of the serpent was what he didn't tell them. He didn't tell them their hearts would be darkened and their moral weakness would leave them vulnerable to evil and the evil one. This was, of course, the means by which Satan gained a foothold in God's good creation. He gained control of humanity through the evil now present in our hearts.

Now it seems we can see good and evil outside ourselves fairly well, but inside it's a different story. Inside we cannot even judge the motives of our own hearts (1 Corinthians 4:4-5). We are smarter than Adam and Eve were before the fall, but we are worse off. We know good and evil, but we cannot control either. We cannot always do the right thing, and we cannot always avoid the wrong thing. In the words of the apostle Paul: "What I want to do I do not do [the good], but what I hate I do [the evil]" (Romans 7:15) Or as Bob Dylan observed, at best we are only serving the Lord over the devil, because everyone has to serve somebody.

Nevertheless, good still remains in the conscience of every human being, and it still is something all people revere and desire. How else can you explain the moral struggle that enters the plot of virtually every story line we come up with? Or how else do you explain the overwhelming propensity for the good to win out? Unless we see people this way and acknowledge that non-Christians desire the good as much as we do, we will forever be misjudging the world around us.

Life on Loan

This is why businesses can be based on biblical principles when no one is committed to Christ. (The most successful businesses usually are.) Peter Drucker, one of the most respected economists and business advisors in the last century, is a Christian who bases his theories on biblical principles. He just doesn't reveal his sources. He is a Christian who has brought truth into the marketplace without waving a Christian flag. There are many more like him in other areas of society. And there are those who have stumbled on the success of the truth as expressed in the Bible without ever finding a personal belief in God or his Son, Jesus Christ. That doesn't make their theories less true.

Thinking in terms of a common grace enjoyed by all and a common good desired by many opens up a myriad of avenues to worship—a worship we do not have to leave the world to partake in. Greek mythology, morality plays, business ethics, movies, and novels that explore the development of human character, and things like sportsmanship in athletics are all components of secular society that contain a good deal of truth that Christians with a Christian worldview can find and endorse. Whether or not we choose to preach God as the source of good in any of these things, we can certainly find and affirm him for ourselves, in our hearts. This is God leaking out into culture, for he is everywhere there is goodness. In other words, we can worship God in the world as the source of all that is good and right and true. When others are only following someone's advice, we recognize that advice as having been borrowed from God. Indeed, we can think of all of life as on loan from him.

I am thinking of a couple lines from that great Isaac Watts hymn, "I Sing the Mighty Power of God": "...while all that borrows life from Thee is ever in Thy care, and everywhere that man can be, Thou, God, art present there."

This is all about inside information. Not everybody knows this. Not everybody is thinking about it. Not many non-Christians know it or even suspect it, and tragically, not many Christians know it either. Christians often miss God in the vision statement of a company, or in the secular novel we are reading and the way the main character is evolving, or in the photographs that adorn the current display in the local art museum, or on the front page of the newspaper we read this morning, or in the TV sitcom we saw last night, or in the instruction manual on how to run the dishwasher....Though life and truth in many of these cases was borrowed from God, many Christians miss it for the simple reason that no one told us to look for him there. We are so used to having God acknowledged when we are supposed to worship him that we fail to see him when his truth comes through other sources. It's time to look not only up, but out, and see God where few expect to see him, in the middle of everything we do.

Even in the Fall

In the publisher's description of a new book by Chris Seay, *The Gospel According to Tony Soprano,* the author is described as examining how this series "provokes us, challenges us, and pries back the exterior to peek into the darkest parts of our souls. The book explores the many reasons why the show has connected so deeply with American culture and exposes the mysteries of life and faith that emerges just behind the curtains of baked ziti and Armani suits."[2]

Most readers will recognize *The Sopranos* as a very popular HBO series that follows the sordid lives and escapades of an Italian mafia family. It is laced with language, violence, and sexual immorality. What could possibly be "gospel" about this? One of the main arguments of the book is that it puts the consequences of sin on display. "The wages of sin is death," said Paul (Romans 6:23), and "God cannot be mocked. People reap what they sow" (Galatians 6:7). This is a show in which the characters reap what they sow. In that manner, at least, God is not mocked.

Now in order for this to be a Christian show, would it have to also include the rest of the verse about the wages of sin: "but the gift of God is eternal life in Christ Jesus our Lord"? Do you need the whole verse to make it truthful or to see God in it? Do we have to have our main character stumble into a Billy Graham crusade meeting and accept Christ before we can see God in this program? If it is true to the first part of the verse (the wages of sin), is it not still true? Does it not confirm a Christian worldview? Indeed, you could say that *The Sopranos* confirms a Christian worldview in that it does not have people getting away with sin. Getting away with sin is a much more dangerous theme. There are numerous PG-13 stories of people getting away with sin while some R-rated films paint sin's true wages, and yet the PG film often gets the Christian nod due to its rating alone. Christians who are not looking beyond ratings for God's truth in the world are venturing into culture's waters in very leaky vessels.

Gustave Flaubert's classic French novel *Madame Bovary* is another story which delves deeply into the consequences of sin; in this case, an adulterous relationship. In terrifying detail the author points out the destruction wrought through selfishness, lies, and infidelity. It's enough to make a person think twice before considering such a liaison. A more modern film rendition of the same theme would be *Fatal Attraction* starring Michael Douglas and Glenn Close. It was reported that some men were actually scared out of adulterous relationships by this movie, much the way *Jaws* cleared a lot of beaches when it first came out.

God and truth can be found in accurate, though painful and sometimes graphic, renditions of the fall. The consequences of sin are explored in the Old Testament in the stories of David, Samson, Gideon, and many others. These stories have both good and evil at war in the hearts of God's servants. The irony of *The Sopranos* is that good is also represented in the intense loyalty and friendship that would make even the ultimate sacrifice for a family member if necessary. Tony Soprano is shown to be a complicated man with good and evil present in his soul, and regular sessions with his psychiatrist bring him no relief.

The Face of God

It is in this exploration of the human soul that we find the highest value in the world around us and the most worthy of praise in the creative expressions of artists who capture it. I am referring to the image of God imprinted on every human being. Regardless of what fell at the fall (and I think it is impossible for us to answer this fully because we have such little knowledge of what we once were), this part remains. We are, all of us, saved and unsaved, made in the image of God. And if we are in the image of God, then God is somehow reflected in every one of us.

Some time ago I gave my wife a book of photographs of women. It is a unique study in black and white of the female character through the eye of a camera and the artist behind it. The subjects cross all ages and social strata and represent a wide variety of ethnic groups, from the weathered face of an aboriginal grandmother to the smooth porcelain skin of a beautiful young Asian movie star. It occurs to me every time I look at this book that it is, among many other things, a study of the face of God.

We still possess the things about us that reflect our Maker. Our senses, our thinking, our will, our emotions—all of these in some way manifest something about God. What happened to the image when we fell? Was it marred beyond recognition? Did Adam and Eve cease to be in the image of God when they walked out of the garden? Were they demoted to some other kind of life form? We have no indication of this kind of alteration. The innocence was lost but not the image. In the same way, the resurrected body of Jesus was not unrecognizable. We have no indication from the disciples that Jesus' appearance after his resurrection was altered in any way. They could even see and touch his wounds.

If this is true, then everyone reflects something about God. I can worship God through the people around me. You can say this almost any way you want and it still remains true: We've all got some of God; we all reflect his glory in some way. "She's got her father's eyes," we say, or "That's his mother's nose." Well, it is the same with our heavenly Father. Even those who are physically or emotionally deformed or handicapped bear the image. Jesus once said, "Whatever you did for one of the least of these brothers and sisters of mine, you did for me" (Matthew 25:40), thus equating himself with the lowliest—the homeless, the sick, the strangers, and the ones in prison. What you do to them, you do to Christ. Well then, are they Christ? The simple answer is that they are to us, for we can see Christ in them. This goes for everybody, even people you hate. (Perhaps if we saw them this way, we might not hate them anymore.)

People are holy. They are, every one of them, in the image of God. No exceptions. To touch someone is to touch the sacred. We are so seldom aware of this, but it remains true nonetheless. We need not wait for the sacred walls and stained-glass windows of the church to draw our gaze upward; we need only to touch the sacred skin that God is in right next to us. Then we will worship God in the beauty of holiness, and in the holiness of people.

All Good Gifts

There are gifts of God that all enjoy. It's a beautiful life, as the movie says, and it is given for all to experience. The difference is that Christians can acknowledge God as the source of all that is good. In the same breath, however, to not acknowledge God as the source of all that is good in this life is to be no different than the unbeliever. "Every good and perfect gift is from above, coming down from the Father of the heavenly lights, who does not change like shifting shadows" (James 1:17). That is a sweeping, unqualified statement. Every experience of anything good in life comes from God, meaning he is to be thanked and worshiped for this. Our praise can issue forth from our hearts continually. Jesus once healed ten lepers, and only one came back and thanked him. The other nine still were healed. They experienced the kindness of God. Those who are experiencing what is good in this life without acknowledging God are like the lepers who were healed and never went back to their healer. Maybe if we keep acknowledging God and giving him thanks, we can lead some of them back.

Tank Tops on the Fourth of July

I close this chapter with a true story that deeply challenged my interpretation of these truths.

Three years ago, we celebrated the Fourth of July in a gay restaurant in Laguna Beach, California, a tourist town with an emphasis on the arts and known to have a high concentration of homosexuals who live in and patronize its businesses. We knew about a couple gay bars in town, but this was the first time I ever encountered a gay restaurant. I didn't even know such a thing existed.

By "we" I mean my wife and I and our ten-month-old son. We didn't realize the sexual orientation of the restaurant until after we had ordered. The realization came upon us slowly because we were among the first patrons that evening, so there was nothing that would have indicated this except perhaps for the fact that they didn't have a high chair for the baby. That seemed odd, given the number of people who bring their children out to dinner these days, but any possible reason for this escaped us. What didn't escape us, however, were the two guys who came in together dressed in silk American-flag tank tops and blue short shorts. As the restaurant continued to fill up, the only patrons who were not same-sex was a couple behind me that looked as though they were visiting from Iowa. My wife gave me a graphic running account of the man's face as reality dawned on him. We noticed they ate and left very quickly.

Now I pride myself in being open-minded, but I must admit I didn't waste much time eating, either. Not only was I nervous by the clientele, but Chandler, our ten-month-old, was making a big scene with the food on the table. Without a high chair, I had to "wear" him in one of those front-facing packs, which put him within striking distance of my plate. It was the only way of controlling him. The food had arrived as a work of art on the plate, and Chandler had decided to continue the creative process. I was continually choosing between the mess of his hands in my food and his screaming every time I tried to pull him away. Adding to my irritation was my wife's apparent enjoyment of my predicament. All I could feel was every eye on us and the audacity of bringing a baby into such a place.

Exasperated and smeared with food from Chandler's grimy hands, I left the bill with Marti and removed myself along with my screaming little attachment. As I waited for her, I could see her talking with two gentlemen seated at the table behind her. They were two who had looked over at our table often, and my original/thoughts towards them are not something I am proud of. I was about to learn a huge lesson in judgment, though. When she finally joined us outside, I asked what her conversation was all about.

"You'll never believe it," she replied as we walked home. "I went over to apologize for interrupting their dinner, and they said, 'Oh no, quite the contrary. We love the sound of a happy baby. You see, my friend and I are retired physicians, and for the last two years we have done nothing but take care of over 6000 battered and abused babies. Believe me, you have a beautiful baby; nothing but music to our ears.'"

I learned a valuable lesson that day. I learned what you miss when you categorize people based on a sin, a mar in the image, or even their unbelief. You miss the beauty in people regardless of their salvation. In fact, it is precisely because of the beauty of the good in people that we long for them to be eternally saved.

SEVEN

Outside In

All dematerialized spiritualities are vacant lots.[1]

EUGENE PETERSON

❖ ❖ ❖

Many Christians today share an incorrect conception of what it means to be pure and set apart from the world. This misconception springs largely from a word in the Scriptures most often translated "sanctified." It primarily means to set something apart for its intended use. The essence of the word has to do with usefulness, not physical separation. You sanctify a book by reading it, not by putting it in a holy place. You sanctify your life by living in a holy way in the middle of the world, not by sequestering yourself in some holy place apart from it. It's an active word. When Jesus prayed about setting us apart in his prayer for all believers in John 17, it is for the purpose of sending us out into the world. Being set apart, then, is something that is meant to take place in the midst of an unsanctified environment.

And yet this idea so often represents the physical act of being removed from the world. The more popular understanding of being set apart today is to be separate, holy, and untainted by the world. In other words, it's an external thing. This kind of approach to holiness resembles the "hear no evil, see no evil, speak no evil" assumptions of Confucianism more than it does the biblical idea of being sanctified. It's a righteousness acquired by cleaning up the spiritual environment a person moves around in.

This is one of the reasons why the Christian market is thriving right now. It deals in tangibles—things you can buy and surround yourself with that can substitute for the world's things and thus stay untainted by the world. This is also why the Christian subculture is largely headed the wrong way—away from the world rather than into it, as Christ sent his followers. We have an idea of holiness that is predominately thought of in terms of externals. We change our lives by changing our environment, our associations, even our friends.

The problem is that this physical separation sounds great and noble on one level, but on another level it is a paradigm that is alienating Christians from the world. The more we keep holiness in the external, the less effective we will be in the world. When you are avoiding the world in order to stay holy, it is hard—almost impossible—to not develop a host of negative attitudes toward the world you are avoiding, such as a general impatience with non-Christians, anger toward sinners, an unforgiving attitude toward certain sins you find abhorrent and threatening to your sense of decency, distaste for the world's art and creative expression, enmity toward individuals who you think are perpetrators of evil, and a fear of those whom you determine are preying on your children. Many cultural Christians today see non-Christians as those who blow secondhand smoke on their smoke-free environments.

How can we possibly go into the world with the love of Christ when we are carrying along these attitudes as baggage? We can't. So we end up withdrawing our faith further into a Christian shell and becoming more separatist in our thinking, judgmental towards others, and convinced the only safe place for us and our loved ones is to be tucked away in a subculture. And believe me, Christian enterprising couldn't be happier. With a Christian alternative to virtually everything in popular culture including breath mints, there is no end in sight for Christian consumerism. Our demand for a better, cleaner, safer world will not go unanswered as long as there is a profit to be made from it.

Editing the World

A perfect illustration of how those who traffic in external values can benefit from making morality culturally tangible can be seen by examining a new Utah-based video house that edits popular Hollywood films for concerned viewers. Clean-Flicks sells already edited versions of many bestselling videos, but it will also clean up any movie you send for $12. That's $12 to eliminate nudity, violence, and bad language from your video monitor. Highly violent movies like *Gladiator* and *The Patriot* cost even more, up to $17 an edit. And now, according to a *Christianity Today* report, another studio will soon release movies with scenes digitally doctored instead of cut. Kate Winslet is no longer topless in *Titanic,* bloody bullet wounds disappear in *The Matrix,* and swords, reminiscent of biblical ploughshares, have been beat into Star Warsian light beams in *The Princess Bride.*

While the success of such an enterprise points out that a significant amount of people are troubled by Hollywood's frequent emphasizing of gratuitous sex, violence, and language, the simple solution of editing these things out poses problems of another kind.

In some ways, the whole industry of contemporary Christian products and services could be seen as a way of editing the world by creating a cleaner, safer version of popular culture for cultural Christians to enjoy. This is an unfortunate way of thinking because of what it robs from the individual Christian: 1) the challenge to think for oneself, 2) the responsibility of discernment, and 3) the opportunity of finding God in the world and a connecting point of truth with non-Christians.

What the "Christian Market" Steals from Christians

Let's look at these ways of thinking one at a time because each is important in having and keeping a vital faith flourishing in the world.

First, the challenge to think for oneself. You shall "love the Lord your God with all your...mind" (Matthew 22:37).

God gave us all a mind, but sometimes I wonder if we aren't trying to give it back. There are so many evidences in cultural Christianity of Christians opting to let someone else think for them. Here are a few indications of what I mean.

The preponderance of large churches getting larger. This is not always the case, but more often than not, the larger church translates to less involvement from individual members. Everything revolves around a charismatic leader who usually has the final word. In a small group, what you think is important; in a large group your thoughts are often irrelevant.

The preponderance of "how-to" books versus "tool" books. How-to books tell you what to do; tool books help you make up your mind about things by providing tools to do that. The overwhelming response I get from readers of my books and articles is that my writing confirms what they were already thinking about. I find great satisfaction in this. That means I don't put ideas into people's heads, I help them think about what is already there. I would never want someone to uncritically adopt my thinking, but I would hope that my thinking might help sharpen theirs.

It's the difference between what to think and how to think. Some teach as if proper Christian education consisted of putting the right things into kids' heads. In her landmark essay, "Tools of Learning," Dorothy Sayers holds that teaching kids how to think for themselves, how to formulate an argument, how to logically state a point of view, and how to make sense of what they believe is far more important than filling their minds with facts and information. Sayers believes that facts and information are simply the raw materials they pick up along the way. What they do with that information is a far more important issue.

This means that as educators, we are often leery of the wrong kid. The one who asks a lot of questions, the one who is always bucking the system, the one who always begins sentences with "Yes, but..." This is most often the kid who is on the right track. The kids who cause the most problems are usually the best learners and the ones who will go on to change their world. The quiet kids who think and do exactly as they are told—the very ones who are often held up as the best examples of behavior—are the ones we should really worry about. Christians have a tendency to equate questioning with rebellion. Questioning is nothing more than brain-breathing. It means someone is still alive in there. Passive compliance rarely translates to personal ownership.

Thus, to automatically assume that a Christian version of something is better for you is incorrect. Christians who uncritically accept the Christian version of culture are letting someone else do their thinking for them.

The second thing that is important to having and keeping a vital faith in the world is to learn the value of discernment. I am always surprised at the number of students I encounter in Christian colleges across the nation who want some kind of ethical line drawn for them in relation to popular culture. They want some authority figure to tell them what movies are okay to watch and what rock groups to stay away from. What alarms me the most about this is that, at their age, no one has cultivated in them the desire and the ability to make up their own minds about these things. They want there to be a line drawn somewhere, and that tells me two things: 1) they want their world to be this easy to organize and 2) they want someone else to organize it for them.

The writer of Hebrews calls this spiritual immaturity. "In fact, though by this time you should be teachers, you need someone to teach you the elementary truths of God's word all over again. You need milk, not solid food! Anyone who lives on milk, being still an infant, is not acquainted with the teaching about righteousness. But solid food is for the mature, who by constant use have trained themselves to distinguish good from evil" (Hebrews 5:12-14).

Milk is predigested food. It has already been broken down into the basic nutrients. All a baby needs to do is suck and swallow. I think of all the Christian products on the market today and wonder how much nursing is going on. It's as though we're providing a predigested world for grown-up spiritual babies. "You don't have to worry about your kids when they listen to Christian music." This is often the assumption about Christian radio. "Just keep your dial tuned in here, and we'll make sure that nothing evil or offensive will enter their minds." Is this the way to develop mature believers who can encounter the world as they know it and make their own decisions about good and evil? Is the purpose of a Christian subculture to provide Christians with an alternative they don't have to think about? This only produces nonthinking, dependent people.

The third consequence to an edited Christian world is that it robs Christians of the opportunity of finding God in the world and a connecting point of truth among non-Christians. This is, in essence, the central premise of this book: that God is at large in the world, and identifying truth from other than Christian sources can help us communicate the gospel to a world that is largely turned-off by a culturally segmented Christianity. Christians who have trained themselves to find truth in the world are not only expanding their own experience of worship, they are finding and gathering a point of reference from which they can dialogue with non-Christians. They are learning to enter the "marketplace of ideas" and use the world's own cultural language to identify truth.

In this regard I often find an insidious hypocrisy at work among many cultural Christians who are not thinking through their own presuppositions. I find, for instance, that when I use secular songs and movies to illustrate a message, Christians know and recognize what I am talking about. These are the same Christians who judge the world as being unfit for believers. They support a Christian subculture, but they are also watching all the popular shows on television and many of the mainstream movies, especially when they come out on video. This means these people are simultaneously judging and indulging in culture. This is simply not healthy. Those who do this are becoming dangerously double-minded and unstable. They are condemning themselves without knowing it and wasting their opportunity to expand their understanding of God and their compassion for a lost world. They are separating themselves from the world in their minds while becoming like it at the same time.

This hypocrisy can be so blind as to judge others for the very thing one is involved in. (Guilt and judgment usually work this way.) When we provide a safe, edited version of the world "for Christians only," we tacitly judge the world as being unfit for believers and we encourage an exodus by Christians from mainstream culture. This creates a sort of antiworld bias among Christians that condemns not only the world but other Christians who choose to openly embrace it. Those who elect to involve themselves as Christians in the world must often suffer the skepticism of these cultural Christians for not sharing their separatist views—hypocritical though they may be. I know of parents who have had their Christian friends tell them they must not love their kids because they are sending them to a public school. Tragically, Christians trying to make a significant difference in the world these days can get more grief from other Christians than they receive from the world.

Why No One Can "Draw the Line"

I've already mentioned the tendency of college-age Christians to want someone to draw a line for them out in the world. This deserves a closer look as it shows how futile it is to think we can change the world from the outside in. This line is usually thought of as a moral limit for a Christian in culture beyond which one is either out-and-out sinning or in a place of compromise where not even the strongest Christian could possibly remain true to Christ—a kind of point of no return for the faithful. You can go this far but no farther. You can go to non-Christian parties but not to bars. You can see "PG-13" movies but not "R" rated movies. Steven Curtis Chapman is okay, but P.O.D. is not.

It is often exasperating for me to receive the "But where do you draw the line?" question because there is so much behind the question that needs reorienting. There is not a one-sentence answer to this. It is an answer that I have come to see has at least three parts.

There is a problem drawing a cultural line anywhere out in the world in the first place because such an attempt focuses only on the external world, and the external world never cooperates that easily with simplistic judgments. This gets us into areas where even Paul refuses to draw a line, preferring to call some things sin to some people and not to others (Romans 14:13-23). Very few things in our cultural experience break down to being simply good or bad, and most of those we already know about. (The Ten Commandments pretty much cover these.) Our cultural experiences, just like our lives, are a complicated tangle of right and wrong, good and evil. Untangling this mess does not conclude with simple labels on things, nor are the conclusions going to be the same for everybody. The real work of untangling the world is a personal issue for every believer, and it should be an ongoing debate among fellow Christians. It takes place primarily in the heart and mind.

Secondly, those who want lines drawn through their world don't want the responsibility of discerning right and wrong for themselves. Even if there were lines out there, I would not want to draw them for anyone else. Cultural lines produce cultural legalism, and legalism always drives Christians away from the world and away from their own responsibilities in the world.

And finally, more often than not, I find that kids who want a line drawn for them out in the world are not primarily motivated out of a true desire for personal holiness. Often, they are only wanting to find out how much of the world they can get away with, or, worse than that, they are hypocritically judging their fellow Christians for what they accuse them of getting away with. The inner attitude is completely skewed. When people ask me, "But John, where do you draw the line?" I assume they are really asking, "How much can I indulge in culture without having to worry about it?" to which I would reply, "You'd better worry about it. Worry about everything you do in the world because your engagement in the world is an integral part of your faith in God. You need to worry, because there is no line and no one can draw it. It does not exist."

What Survives the Cutting Floor

This is precisely why the CleanFlicks editing enterprise I discussed earlier is so inadequate to fulfill its promise to make movie viewing safe for value-oriented people. Violence, nudity, and bad language may be cut out, but the bigger questions concern what remains, because the implication is that the movie is now "clean." What goes unexplored in this and other attempts at editing the world is the intrinsic legitimacy or illegitimacy of the things we are copying and editing in the first place. It's as if we've created a decaffeinated world without ever bothering to consider the value of drinking coffee to begin with. And herein lies the greatest danger: By marketing a culture as edited for Christians, we are tacitly approving everything that survived the cutting floor.

For instance, Christian music now has its own Christian stars glorified by their smashing good looks, their professional entourage, and their glitzy ad campaigns. What's been changed? The lyrics, primarily. They are mostly about God and living the Christian life. We hope the lifestyles of the singers are commendable (this is not always the case) so that they are positive role models as well. But their music, and the package it is delivered in, shows the same idolization common in the world.

Whenever we talk about a contemporary Christian editing of culture in any way, the largely overlooked question is not what to edit; it is what doesn't get edited. What are we swallowing whole in our culture, thinking all along that we have the safe version of it? Maybe the bad language has been removed from these movies, but what about the materialism, the self-indulgence, the personal autonomy, the glorification of money, position, and power, or the relativistic truth that permeates Hollywood, such as "Do what your heart tells you to do"? I worry that the ideals the Christian community is carelessly buying from the world are far more dangerous and insidious than the scenes and the language that are edited out.

C.S. Lewis once wrote that it is not overt books on materialism that make a person a materialist; it is the materialistic assumptions in all the other books. In the same light, what assumptions are we inadvertently adopting from the world around us in our "safe" Christian subculture? What gets passed through the sieve of our editing process?

In Jesus' words to the Pharisees, "You strain out a gnat but swallow a camel" (Matthew 23:24). Take the bad language out of a bad movie and you still have a bad movie. You can digitalize a corset on a nude Kate Winslet, but you can't digitalize certain values into the story that are not there to begin with.

We run into problems when we assume that the culture can somehow be detached from the world and made wholly safe. From the beginning, the whole point of Christian music—which has now expanded into every area of cultural expression—was to present a Christian message and witness to the world relevant to contemporary culture. If we are going to create and present something attractive to the world, we cannot be naive to the worldly attraction that accompanies the venue. This was not as much of a problem when our audience was the world (that is, the rebellious dress and music of early Christian rock groups that played well on the streets but not so well in church). But a shift has occurred from being relevant in order to reach the world to being acceptable in order to entertain cultural Christians. This shift has complicated the mission, making it difficult, in some cases impossible, to please both these audiences at the same time. Larry Norman's rock and roll was an offense to established Christianity in 1970. That was a given. But Larry wasn't singing to Christians. We have an audience now that did not even exist 30 years ago.

I recently heard of a student who was kicked out of a Bible college for having a life-size poster of a spaghetti-strapped female diva in his room. The administration judged the suggestive look and the bare shoulder as being inappropriate for Christian males. The irony is in the fact that the person represented is a Christian artist and the poster was created for the local Christian bookstore. Trying to create a safe, culturally relevant Christian world is going to continually pose problems like this.

Can pop culture be made safe for Christians? I think it is highly doubtful. And even if it could be done, it's a bad idea. It makes Christians leave the job of interpreting the world around them to someone else. It removes us one step further away from a world we are here to reach and recover for Christ. The more we depend on these preedited Christian products, the less tolerant we are of the world and the less able to function in it as knowledgeable, compassionate representatives of the gospel.

We have an industry supposedly doing what every Christian needs to be good at: exercising a God-given mind in the pursuit of God and truth in the world. Harry Blamires, author of *The Christian Mind*, lamented in that book the absence of a Christian mind. He may be right. Or at least if there is a Christian mind, it is too lazy to take on the world. Our cultural thinking is much too flabby because a Christian culture excuses us from this task. The truth of the matter is, the Christian mind is a much better editor than any film critic with a knife.

If we are going to indulge in popular culture, it would be much better to interact with the real one we already have than to create a supposedly safe alternative to it. The alternative is neither safe nor important when it comes to why we are Christians in the world.

In the end, nothing is safe in this world. Christians need to be discerning of everything they consume. Christian products are perhaps even the most dangerous because they come with a false assumption of safety. Wouldn't we be better off either dealing with, or rejecting entirely, the world as it is?

Fighting the Wrong Fight

Before leaving the subject of trying to change the world from the outside in, I feel compelled to address the issue of spiritual warfare as it has been so often applied to societal issues in America today. It is my belief that great harm has been done to the opportunity for the gospel in the world by creating cultural enemies in the minds of Christians that do not exist in the real world. We Christians are great at erecting straw men and then surreptitiously knocking them down in the name of Christ.

Paul puts spiritual warfare in terms of intangible evil forces in heavenly places; we, on the contrary, have made our enemies very real. The enemies of Christians have become feminists, Darwinists, abortionists, homosexuals, peaceniks, and most Democrats—in other words, all the people who we perceive as standing against the values we cherish as cultural Christians. This bias once found expression in the monologue of a Christian comedian who quipped, "There are a lot of misconceptions about what it means to be a born-again Christian. It's pretty simple, really. You just bow your head, say a simple prayer, and when you open your eyes you're a registered Republican with a firearm."[2] This would be funnier if it weren't so true.

Over the last 30 years, the "Christians against the world" position has gained a good deal of strength in the Christian community. It is a position that has made us enemies of the world and made the world our enemy. The arguments taken to support this position have remained pretty much the same. They are as follows:

1. The country has gone to pot.

2. We stood by and watched it happen.

3. There's a conspiracy out there against our kids and our values. We've got to stop it.

4. We've got to get this country back to where it was 50 years ago.

5. Those who disagree with any of this are weak, lily-livered do-nothings.

I'd like to follow this up with a by-the-numbers rebuttal of each of these arguments to show that there might be another way to look at them. These arguments may be very effective at creating the fear and anger necessary to get that nonprofit cash flowing, but they are and have been detrimental to the real purposes of Christ in the world.

1. The country has gone to pot. True. Although there is still good in the world. Elements remain in the public sector that Christians can acknowledge. In fact, by joining these instead of condemning the whole thing, we can hold back the tide of corruption by being salt and light in the world.

2. We stood by and watched it happen. True, but not in the way this argument is usually presented. We lost our voice in society not because we did nothing politically but because we left the culture and the public sector in general a long time ago. The very thing this position usually advocates— pulling our kids out of public schools—is one of the reasons why public schools are what they are today. Doesn't it seem self-defeating to take Christian students, Christian teachers, Christian administrators, and Christian parents out of public schools and then justify our leaving by how bad these schools are? The same thing can be applied to television, radio, music, politics, business, law, and so on.

3. There's a conspiracy out there against our kids and our values. We've got to stop it. False. Christian leaders who try and incite the Christian public to action often pit gays, pornographers, and Girl and Boy Scout leaders as those who are attacking our kids. More often than not, these people are not after our kids as much as they are after the right to pursue their own interests, evil and sinful as they might be. This is America, a country founded on personal liberty, and anyone has a right to raise their flag and push the system as far as it will go. Because some of these issues are morally wrong and not the freedoms this country was founded on, they need to be debated and resisted in the courts and legal arenas, but not by provoking fear and anger in the Christian community and further polarizing Christians against the world. This may not be the America the founding fathers envisioned, but this is America, nonetheless, and our freedom implies that our ancestors fought for the freedom of those who disagree with us as well.

4. *We've got to get this country back to where it was 50 years ago.* False. Impossible. This is an entirely different world than it was 50 years ago. You can never go back because the influences have all changed. Besides, the family values so often espoused by those who look longingly back were not the result of people's inner beliefs anyway. That was the way the culture was—the way people were brought up. We can only move forward, taking into account the influences that have shaped our current age (postmodernism, political correctness, consumerism, and so on). It will take a new approach to be Christians in a place of influence in our culture. Old wineskins cannot hold new wine for very long (Matthew 9:17). Solomon lamented that each generation forgets what the former one learned (Ecclesiastes 1:11). We might wish it were different but it is not. Only those who remember can go back, but they are no longer in the places of power and influence. The younger ones who are the next generation do not even know what it is that the old want them to go back to. This is not okay, but it is the way it is. Solomon would agree with me. The arguments have to be re-formed for each new generation.

5. *Those who disagree with any of this are weak, lily-livered do-nothings.* False. Those who disagree might also believe there are other ways to "stem the tide" of moral decline in the country that will not create as many enemies in the world.

They might also believe these other ways are more effective in the long run at changing people and culture. The remainder of this book will be, in fact, an exploration of some of these very ways.

EIGHT

Inside Out

Once, having been asked by the Pharisees when the kingdom of God would come, Jesus replied, "The kingdom of God does not come with your careful observation, nor will people say, 'Here it is,' or 'There it is,' because the Kingdom of God is within you."

LUKE 17:20-21 NIV

❖ ❖ ❖

On any given day in the world, unless we choose a monastic existence, we will be hearing evil and seeing evil. This does not mean we will end up speaking evil or that evil has to gain a foothold in our life. It does mean, however, that we have a job to do interpreting all that we see and hear in light of our faith and the truth on which it stands.

The apostle Paul spoke of this responsibility when he said, "For you were once darkness, but now you are light in the Lord. Live as children of light (for the fruit of the light consists in all goodness, righteousness and truth) and find out what pleases the Lord. Have nothing to do with the fruitless deeds of darkness, but rather expose them. It is shameful even to mention what the disobedient do in secret. But everything exposed by the light becomes visible—and everything that is illuminated becomes a light" (Ephesians 5:8-13).

Our light functions best in the darkness. It is made for this. We do not hide our light and only bring it out when we get together with all the other lights in church. Our light shines in the darkness, and we are asked to do more than just shine it as our own personal possession. We are asked to do a very brave thing with it: to bring to light the fruitless deeds of darkness. In other words, we have been given a moral responsibility with the light we have. This is more than avoidance of the darkness; this assumes, in fact, a certain amount of engagement—enough to expose the error and turn it into something good. It is all about penetrating the darkness with the light of truth.

The light we possess is very clearly explained here. It consists in "all goodness, righteousness and truth." So to expose something bad is not only to point out its badness, but to turn it into something good that can even become a light in someone else's life. This is what it means to illuminate everything, and it is your mission and mine to do so, should we choose to accept it.

Christians have traditionally been good at trying to accomplish the first part of this challenge, and that is to have nothing to do with the fruitless deeds of darkness. At times it has been considered a cultural mandate to ignore the world—to stay as far away from it as possible. Years ago, this would have been what made Christians cultural nerds— when the fruitless deeds of darkness were interpreted as wearing makeup, showing ankles, going to the theater, or playing cards. Now Christians may be more culturally hip, with even our own version of what the world enjoys, but we still are not tackling the job of exposing the darkness in the world. We still keep our cultural distance.

Paul's charge to have nothing to do with the deeds of darkness cannot mean what it first appears to mean. To tell someone to have nothing to do with something would mean don't go near it, don't see it, don't think about it, don't talk about it…act as if it doesn't exist. But this cannot be what Paul means because of his next statement, "but rather expose them." Oddly enough, in order to expose something you have to have something to do with it. You have to shine your light on it or bring it into the light. I am assuming Paul has in mind our own deeds of darkness first. This light is not a handheld flashlight we put on everyone but ourselves. In either case you face the darkness and you illuminate it. You make what was hidden in the darkness light, so you, and everyone around you, can see what is wrong but also see what is possible when we reclaim what is right about something. That is not avoiding darkness; that is making light of it.

Physical Kid

Just yesterday I was speaking with a talented 20-something Christian who was lamenting this very thing. He was challenging me to write something in defense of being a healthy, physical, sexual single man. Here you have a bright, attractive young man loaded with talent and initiative. He has designed numerous album and book covers and has had his original paintings in major galleries. His latest project was to design and decorate a coffee bistro in a high-traffic tourist area. He designed the whole thing—floor to ceiling, kitchen to front door—he even put his own paintings on the wall. He came up with a new line of coffee and coffee drinks. He built the place, decorated it, opened it up to the public, and operated it for nine months. He spoke of all this as something he did just for the fun of it—as if he didn't have anything better he could think of to do with his last nine months. I saw his work. I had visited the shop earlier that day before I met him. All I can say is, "Move over, Starbucks..." The place is very handsome and pleasing to the eye. I wanted to do one thing when I walked in the door—I wanted to sit down in one of the padded chairs and enjoy a cup of java and a good newspaper. It's very obvious this guy is going places. And, as a result, he is going to be around some very creative people, and in his area of design and art, he is going to be found attractive by males and females he associates with in the world. Oh yes, and there's one more thing about him. He is a deeply passionate Christian bent on finding out with his life what pleases the Lord. Now what is he to do?

Well, seeing how Christians have dealt with this issue so far, he has two choices. He can become a eunuch or get married. Short of that, he has to treat his sexuality as if it didn't exist, and this in the most virile years of his life. Suddenly I'm envisioning one of those carnival games where you try to hammer that little stuffed groundhog back into his hole. Of course, as soon as you do, he pops up somewhere else. No one ever wins that game.

Maybe we should ship him off to Africa as a missionary to some distant tribe. Probably wouldn't be the first time someone did this for the wrong reason. The problem is: Here is a talented man who has unlimited opportunities to enter the world as a significant Christian. But how are we helping him? Where is the Christian book about positive sexuality for the single person? Is a cold shower the only advice we can offer him? And this is not even beginning to address the bigger questions of where an artistically motivated Christian can find a church or Christian network of people that can even begin to understand and help him grapple with the issues he will be facing as a professional in the world of secular art and design.

He explicitly told me to write something about this. He said he was thinking about writing it himself. He already has a title for it: Physical Kid. What he is seeking is something positive about his situation including his sexuality—that is, something positive about being an artistically talented 20-something single man without denying he is a sexual being.

My friend's dilemma is a direct result of Christians only hearing half of Paul's admonition. There are plenty of voices to tell this man to have nothing to do with the deeds of darkness when it comes to his sexuality, but not many that can help him expose those deeds and bring out "all goodness, righteousness and truth" about being a sexual being.

I am aware of a handful of writings that might touch on his dilemma and give him hope. One of them is found in a couple of chapters in one of my first books, *Real Christians Don't Dance*. Another comes from an essay I collected from

Theology Today, written by Michael J. McClymond, Ph.D., titled "The Last Sexual Perversion." It is an excellent piece that takes a stab at an encouraging word to single people who abstain from sex but still have a handle on their sexuality. Most Christian books on the subject can only provide some sort of emotional and mental castration as relief. This can't be right for a child of God who has been given all good gifts. McClymond, a single man himself, begins by lamenting a singles scene that treats celibacy as some sort of disease. Then he begins a rather convincing argument that stops short of browbeating.

> A good case can be made for extramarital celibacy. Those who abstain from sex are not "joyless, under-sexed, anti-life, anti-youth, and anti-progress," as alleged. In fact, in the long run, they may be enhancing their erotic life considerably. The arguments, when carefully considered, suggest that celibacy is preferable to promiscuity or a series of transient sexual liaisons. This should not be taken to mean that celibacy is an unmixed blessing. Among other things, celibacy involves the forfeiting of pleasure, and this is negative per se. Some celibate persons may experience psychological and physical symptoms that range from irritability to insomnia or low spirits. Sexual deprivation never killed anyone, to be sure, but this does not mean that someone's general sense of well-being is not diminished by celibacy. Yet, having said this, celibacy outside of marriage is preferable to promiscuity and its associated jealousy, guilt, hurt, and general deadening of emotional sensibility. While the pains of celibacy can soon be forgotten, the wounds of promiscuity may linger for a lifetime.[1]

Later in his article, McClymond quotes writer Kathleen Norris, noting that "celibacy is not a private spiritual attainment, as both Catholics and non-Catholics have often imagined, but rather a form of service to others. 'When you can't make love physically,' says Norris, 'you figure out other ways to do it.' Friendship, in the fullest sense of the word, plays a major role in the lives of most celibate people. They are good friends and have good friends."[2]

Is God the ultimate killjoy, or is he the orchestrater of a massive moving symphony, complete with long sections of lonely oboe solos contrasted by blaring bombastic horns and lyrical dances? Is this a one-night stand or a lifetime of worship? Is God to be trusted, and can I trust him with my most intimate needs and desires? These are the bigger questions for which even our strong sexual urges can and will find answers when we bring to light what has been hidden.

This is by no means the end of this discussion, but it does begin to show how one can expose the darkness by shining light on what is good. If my job is to find out what pleases the Lord, then part of that would be to find out what pleases the Lord about my sexuality. After all, sex was his idea. He gave it to his creation as a gift. He declared it good. He built it into all living things he created: plant, animal, and human. Did he do this just to frustrate? I think not. There is a light that will reveal the answers to these and other related questions, and you have it if you are a child of God. "Everything exposed by the light becomes visible—and everything that is illuminated becomes a light" (Ephesians 5:13).

An Inside Job

What I'm talking about here is an inside job. Not a sanctioning of something on the outside, as we discussed in the last chapter, but an illumination—a way of looking at the world—from within. This is not some Christian expert or institution making the world safe for us, this is the personal, individual responsibility of each of us to find what is true and right and sacred about our human experience. We can get help with this along the way, but we ultimately have to do this work ourselves.

As we found in the previous chapter, we are always tempted to accept someone else's version of this—and there are plenty of sanctioned views of the world available for a price in the Christian market—but that is a rearranging of the world from the outside in. This is different. This is an inside-out job, and because it comes from within, it affects everything we see and do. I am talking about a way of seeing that makes everything sacred.

The Pharisees in the time of Jesus were experts at external sanctification. They had their world and their experience of it all cleaned up by a long list of rules and regulations they believed made everything holy. Jesus had much to say about this.

> Then some Pharisees and teachers of the law came to Jesus from Jerusalem and asked, "Why do your disciples break the tradition of the elders? They don't wash their hands before they eat!" (Matthew 15:1-2).

> Jesus called the crowd to him and said, "Listen and understand. What goes into your mouth does not defile you, but what comes out of your mouth, that is what defiles you" (Matthew 15:10-11).

And when the disciples asked for further explanation, he said,

> Don't you see that whatever enters the mouth goes into the stomach and then out of the body? But the things that come out of the mouth come from the heart, and these defile you. For out of

> the heart come evil thoughts, murder, adultery,
> sexual immorality, theft, false testimony,
> slander. These are what defile you; but eating
> with unwashed hands does not defile you
> (Matthew 15:17-20).

It's a poignant picture, is it not? Pharisees with hearts full
of deceit washing their hands and feeling smug about their
cleanliness. But we do the same thing when we fail to deal
with things from the inside.

On another occasion Jesus spoke to the Pharisees,

> Make a tree good and its fruit will be good, or
> make a tree bad and its fruit will be bad, for a
> tree is recognized by its fruit. You brood of
> vipers, how can you who are evil say anything
> good? For out of the overflow of the heart the
> mouth speaks. Good people bring good things
> out of the good stored up in them, and evil
> people bring evil things out of the evil stored up
> in them (Matthew 12:33-35).

It's an inside job all the way. We are what we are on the
inside. What we think about—how we view the world—
makes up who we are. We can sanctify ourselves and the
world around us by the way in which we see it. Or like the
Pharisees, we can pride ourselves by what we think we look
like on the outside, when all along we are as defiled as the
next guy on the inside. How you see is ultimately more
important than what you see, or perhaps it should be: How
you see determines what you see.

The Enemy of the Best

We have already looked at a number of reasons why the
Christian subculture has been detrimental to the growth of a
Christianity that can engage culture and produce a Christian

who can find truth in the wider world, recovering the essence of what God has created. The Christian subculture deals largely with what happens outside us. But providing "sanctified versions" of everything in the world has not helped Christians learn how to see all things in a sanctified way.

It's ironic and in some ways tragic that the things we thought would help us have hurt us so much. The tragedy is that many people will not notice the danger of a Christian subculture because of the helpfulness of much of which has been created and because of the goodness of the intent.

Christian music helps us worship. Christian radio connects us with other believers and gives us reminders that help us think about God all day long. Christian fiction entertains us with values that are noble. Christian bookstores are cities of refuge in a hostile world where one can find like-minded believers and numerous helps for faith and practical living. Then there are the jobs the Christian subculture has provided for believers who sincerely want to make a lasting difference in the world, and the platforms it has erected for those, including myself, who might not otherwise have an audience.

There is no doubt that many believers have been helped by Christian products and services, and many others have been introduced to Christ by way of these things. There is also the knowledge that the infrastructure that services Christians through popular media, products, and services is not going to go away any time soon, regardless of what I or anyone else says or thinks. In fact, the sales and marketing of Christian products are increasing—one of the few industries actually growing in difficult economic times.

Having said all this, however, it must still be stated that the Christian subculture can be dangerous to faith. We have already looked at some of the reasons for this, but there is one we haven't discussed yet. That danger comes in the form of what C.S. Lewis has referred to as the good being the enemy of the best. The Christian subculture can be shown to be good and valuable, but is it the best? Is it possibly hindering something better?

In an Internet article titled "Getting Out of the Faith Ghetto," Dan Buck observed that much of the Christian subculture is merely "adding spiritual language into things that are actually spiritual because they are part of the human experience God has created."[3] The operative words here being things that are "actually spiritual."

The reason the spiritual language of the subculture is so dangerous is that if we think it is the language, or some other mystical/spiritual connection or blessing inherent in a Christian thing that has made it sanctified, then we lose our drive and need to find God outside the confines of what qualifies for the Christian label. We start to trust the labels and not flex our own spiritual muscle. We are not training ourselves to find God wherever we look—whatever we are doing. In fact, we are actually training people to distrust everything that does not carry the label. We are no longer looking for God; we are counting on someone else to provide him for us in terms relevant to our culture.

The tragedy is that there was something Christian about aerobics before someone thought of Christian aerobics; there was something Christian about music before there was Christian music; there was something Christian about people connecting on the radio and in stores before we had Christian radio and Christian bookstores. But now that we have "Christian" so clearly defined, it makes it harder to find God anywhere else. We assume the language or the association makes it Christian and stop using our inner spiritual eyes to find God and his truth in other ways. It is similar to kosher food needing the sanction of the rabbi when the food that was given by God was good already. This is downsizing the truth by defining it and promising it to people by way of a Christian market.

Even if all this Christian stuff really is good, it remains to be not a good idea. What would be better would be Christians who can worship God while watching anything, when walking into any store, while reading any book, and pursuing any vocation. The best would be to not have more great Christian things but more people who are great Christians without needing Christian things to define them or help them along.

The good is not the enemy of the best until it becomes a substitute for it. If you pursue what is best, the good is no threat—it may even be useful in a limited sort of way—but if the good is all you have, or if it masks itself as the best, then you are impoverished. You become like the Pharisees who thought they could see when they really couldn't. The Christian subculture may be good, but it is ultimately not a good idea when it comes to Christians living in and relating to the world. It is simply not all that is Christian about the world. It makes for a very narrow worldview.

What You See Is What You Get

Instead of handing God to people in a defined Christian wrapping, we could be showing them how to find him at large. Instead of delivering God to people in a Christian package, we could be pointing to him where he already is, in that which they already know and experience. Instead of saying, "Here he is," we could say, "There he is."

Ever notice how people want to find out what the big deal is if they come upon someone staring up—how they gather around and stare too? Actually, it doesn't have to be up. It could be down or out or anywhere for that matter. The operable thing seems to be the intent. If you are intently looking somewhere, people will look along with you. They want to know what could possibly be so important to have captured your attention. It's human nature. When people look at us looking at him, they start to look in that direction too.

Besides, saying "Here he is" has the arrogance of finality about it. It seems to say we have all of him here. "There he is" carries the idea of worship—something too big to contain. We can see him there...and there...and there...and—oh look, he's over there too! Wait a minute, suddenly he's every-where!

This is, I believe, what Paul had in mind when he said "To the pure, all things are pure" (Titus 1:15). This is like saying "To the baseball fanatic, everything comes up looking like baseball." It has to do with your inner focus. What you are like indicates what you are going to see. Perhaps we can see this more clearly if we look at it the other way around. A man who fills his mind with pornographic images of women is going to have difficulty looking on women in purity, seeing their inner beauty, marveling at their intelligence, and connecting with their spirit. He has trained himself to use the female form as an object for erotic stimulus, and because his view is skewed, all women become objects to him. Or take someone who is suspicious of everyone. Is it any wonder that everyone that person meets is suspect? It's a fairly simple self-fulfilling prophecy. To the fearful, everything is scary. To the judgmental, everyone is passing judgment. To the con man, everyone is crooked.

Now let's go back to the pure in heart. This person can't see anything but that which is pure. She trusts, she believes, she hopes to see God, and she is not disappointed. Her inner life directs her outward vision. Someone who is full of mercy is merciful. Someone full of grace is gracious. I always think of Mother Teresa when I ponder this verse in Titus. She had a way of seeing that always had Christ in view. Those who were ugly to most people were beautiful to her. Every person was Christ for her. When serving the poor and the helpless, she always felt she was touching and handling Jesus himself.

Thus, though a pure world will never exist in our mortal lifetime, one with pure eyes sees it so. Purity becomes a personal possession, not an outward definition or identity.

Nowhere is this concept more clearly stated than in Christ's Sermon on the Mount: "Blessed are the pure in heart, for they will see God" (Matthew 5:8). This statement is so obvious I missed it for years. I don't know why, but for some reason I always read a future tense into it. The pure in heart will see God...someday. It doesn't say that. I conferred with an expert in biblical languages, who affirmed what I was beginning to suspect. The verb tense translated into English as "will see God" doesn't express time only in the future, but a general principle that is true at any time. That puts this verse squarely in the "inside out" camp along with these others. The pure in heart see God. Where? Everywhere. When? Now. The pure in heart walk around seeing God.

A desire to be able to see God is a strong incentive for moral purity as well. It gives us a positive reason for self-control. This thought (that impurity will obscure my vision of God) more than any other has helped me to deal with sexual lust. I ask myself: "Do I really want this thought, or do I want to see God?" I have seen this work over and over in my life, though it is not a battle I always win. It definitely beats beating up on oneself over bad thoughts. Thus it is morally and spiritually true: What you see is what you get. Our inner vision determines the world we walk around in. This is why it is fruitless and counterproductive to real spiritual growth to try and make the outside world conform to our ideals, as good as they may be.

Kinkade's World: Light or Painter of Light?

Paul completes his thoughts on the subject of exposing the darkness with the following: "Be very careful, then, how you live—not as unwise but as wise, making the most of every opportunity, because the days are evil" (Ephesians 5:15-16). Once again, this does not appear to be a retreat from the world. Quite the opposite. "Making the most of every opportunity" is another positive incentive to see and take advantage of the value of our place in the world. We know Paul is talking about the world here because "the days are evil," and yet that is all the more reason to make the most of each situation. His admonition places Christians squarely in the midst of an evil world as redemptive factors.

This contrasts what I frequently hear from Christians. When Christians talk about their involvement in the world, be it work or school or neighborhood, they rarely speak of it as an "opportunity" or something they look forward to. More often than not, it is an obligation to somehow endure. We like to complain about how evil the world is and how much we begrudge having to be in it. Indeed, much of the impetus for a Christian subculture is fed by the thought of escaping all this. Given Paul's admonition to redeem the time in the evil days we live in, this is most unfortunate.

It makes me think of Thomas Kinkade, Christian "Painter of Light," who has met with overwhelming success in and out of the Christian subculture. I am not an art critic, and I have no desire to be one. I do know something about theology and the Scriptures, however, and I cannot help observing a connection between Kinkade's own description of his paintings and their success, especially in the Christian market. For by his own admission, Kinkade has said that he paints life without the fall. I suppose that's an interesting thing to speculate about, but is it really helpful? Is it even life? Certainly it is not life as we know it, because we are all fallen and live in a fallen world. It's like saying, "I paint life on Mars." Well, that's fine, but no one can get there. We need to learn how to redeem life in a fallen world, not how to surround ourselves with comforting images of a world that does not exist.

In order to have "light" in Kinkade's paintings there has to be darkness too, but even this darkness is unlike the world's. It is virtually harmless—usually twilight at dusk or dawn. Kinkade's world has no evil in it. That means the light in his paintings is not a true light because it doesn't expose anything. Christians are called to expose deeds of darkness, not create a false world where even darkness is benign. I fear these images, as beautiful as they may be, are merely mirroring a Christian subculture that doesn't even get darkness right.

We are called to face a dark world with the light of Christ. That light comes from his presence in our hearts, and it will be found as he permeates our vision from within, until everything we see is somehow touched by it.

Tired of the Light

The Painter of Light could be contrasted with another Christian artist who has by her own admission grown tired of light. "The stage is empty and tired of light," sings Sam Phillips in the title song of her 2002 album, *Fan Dance*. I have a feeling Sam would look into those warm, radiant houses at twilight and see dysfunctional families, lies, worries, financial problems, broken marriages, sexual immorality, sickness, disease, conflicts, and strife. She would know that even the best of Christian homes are not exempt from any of these things. And Sam, as a Christian, would want to paint this, or in her case, sing about it. And her work would be no less Christian than Kinkade's.

Sam is a Christian artist who left Christian music to pursue what she felt to be a more honest approach to her music. Her story is unique in that with one person we have two careers and two entirely different settings for those careers—even two names. She was Leslie Phillips in her Christian career. Now she is Sam Phillips. Two names, two markets, two incarnations of the same talent. It's a unique opportunity for comparison. Leslie was dogmatic; Sam is ambiguous. Leslie was positive; Sam is gloomy. Leslie was all about shining the light; Sam is about describing the darkness. Leslie was safe; Sam is controversial. Leslie sang to cultural Christians. Sam sings for anybody.

These two stages also make it easy to compare two different ways in which a Christian artist can approach her work. One is to express herself in an arena where her Christianity is overt. In this setting, hope is paramount. Faith messages predominate, and Christ is presented as the answer to our human predicament. Happiness has the last word. Conflict and struggle can enter the picture, but they ultimately lead to a positive conclusion. Here, stories have happy endings. These are unwritten rules and unspoken expectations. Christian art is all about light, warmth, and goodness.

"The stage is empty and tired of light." Is it possible to be tired of light? I think it is, if we have not in some way embraced the darkness. The light has to shine somewhere to be truly meaningful in our lives, not just shine out from a stage. Sooner or later the stage goes empty, and who is going to sing about that? Leslie couldn't but Sam can. Perhaps Sam got tired of the bright stage of Christian music and wanted to explore what happens when the lights go off and everyone goes home—in some cases to houses where the light is not on at all.

It's a tragedy she felt she had to leave Christian music in order to do this with integrity, because it is what Paul has asked us to do (expose the darkness), but Christian music has never provided much of a home to Christians who felt it necessary to embrace the more negative aspects of the human experience.

Sam's music is not entirely devoid of light. Indeed, sometimes light can be more powerful when it is cast into the dark corners of our lives. That's what these artists do, and for that reason, perhaps it is best that they remain on the outside of Christian music, where their work can be more appreciated and their truth can be more effective. That which often brings criticism in the Christian marketplace can end up bringing hope in the world.

NINE

Worship in Everyday Life

Therefore I urge you, brethren, by the mercies of God, to present
your bodies a living and holy sacrifice, acceptable to God,
which is your spiritual service of worship.

ROMANS 12:1 NASB

❖ ❖ ❖

Jennifer feels she is really worshiping when two or three of her favorite worship songs are strung together, each one taking her higher than the one before. Robert's passion for Christ soars on the third verse of "And Can It Be That I Should Gain?" Tanya doesn't feel as though she is really reaching God until the decibel level reaches sonic boom proportions. Vincent will tell you that God only gets through to him in the silence. Irene thinks angels sing in the organ pipes. What do these people all have in common? They are worshiping God. How much of this worship experience will carry over to Monday morning? That's a good question.

Never before, at least in my lifetime, has worship been more important to Christians; and never before has it been more complicated and tentative, as people shuffle from church to church seeking the right blend of worship experience for their families in what seems like an endless zero-sum game. Statistics show that larger churches are not necessarily growing by converts; they are just better at more popular forms of worship, siphoning off the attendance from smaller churches that simply can't keep up the level of professionalism these larger churches can command. Even what used to be the all-important sermon now seems more an adjunct to praise and worship. People go to church today to experience God more than they go to hear about him.

We live in a postmodern age that has come to value intuition over reason, and experience over just about everything. Nothing can really be trusted today except one's feelings, and worship, as it is commonly believed, is more than anything a feeling. Churches that cater to that feeling unwittingly support the notion that worship is the church's business. You come to church for what you can't find anywhere else, a corporate experience of worshiping God. For many Christians it is their only experience of worshiping God. This should not be the case. People can worship without music, without professional worship leaders, and without a church service to prompt and guide them, but too few know how.

A New Standard

Thirty years ago it was enough to reason God's existence. If faith could be shown to be rational, people would believe. But people don't want to talk about God now as much as they want to experience him. Nothing I know captures this shift in thinking better than two popular book titles about searching for God—Francis Schaeffer's landmark philosophical work of the late 1960s, *The God Who Is There,* and Bill Hybels' equally significant offering roughly 30 years later, *The God You're Looking For.* So what if God is there? Is he here? Can I meet him? Can I encounter him in my life? The God people are looking for today is a God they can experience, and they experience him primarily through what we now call praise and worship.

The good thing about this shift is that it seems more people are willing to assume God is there. This assumption reflects a general spiritual hunger in our society. Spiritual themes are now common even in popular culture, and church attendance is up. The bad thing about this is that each person now becomes the sole and final authority as to what worship is: that is, worship is what connects with me. What I like and understand is what ministers to me. Personal preference becomes sacred ground, forcing a people's corporate experience with God to be made up of individual personal connections.

Worship ends up being something that happens to someone, and something that happens only in church. The church that "does it best" is the church that relates to someone personally. It has become the church's responsibility to lead people into worship instead of everyone's responsibility to worship God regardless. If the church were made up of people who were translating the love and experience of God into everyday life, it wouldn't be so important how the church "did" worship.

Mind on God

God is after a life of worship for each one of us. It's what Paul calls our "service of worship" (Romans 12:1 NASB)—presenting ourselves to him continually as living sacrifices, transformed in our thinking and awake to his will in the world (Romans 12:2). Unfortunately, we have turned this service of worship (which takes up our whole life) into a worship service (which takes up about an hour a week).

We worship not because it's Sunday, not because our favorite style of music is inducing us to think about God, but because we are worshipers. We were created with a big cavity inside our souls that can't be filled with anything but God, and filling ourselves with God on a continual basis is the most fulfilling thing we can do. It is what we were made for. Yes, it incorporates our emotions—sometimes more than other times—but that is not nearly all there is to worship. True worship incorporates our minds in understanding, our strength in service, our souls in wonder, and our spirits in praise. It does not take a song to do this. It takes my mind on God and my whole being focused in his direction.

Worship is something that can go along with everything else we normally do; in fact, it is what gives everything else meaning. This is what Paul meant when he said to do everything we do to the glory of God (1 Corinthians 10:31). It's a life, not a worship service, that will make us worshipers. We don't go to church to worship, we go to church because we are already worshipers. And if someone is a true worshiper—which means their whole life is an act of worship—then what happens in church is a very small part of the whole.

I often hear people say they think they need to give God more of their time. Longer quiet time, more prayer, more Bible reading. All well and good, but I'm not so sure it's more of my time God wants as much as he wants more of my attention. It's not this time over here for God, and this time over there for work, and this time for play, and this time for me. It's the whole thing for God. All or nothing at all. If we see this correctly, the way I believe God wants us to see, then everything we do is sacred, and all of life is an act of worship.

Everywhere I Go I See You

One of the most important statements on worship to come from Jesus happened in the middle of a highly unusual conversation he had with a Samaritan woman at the well of Jacob. "Our ancestors worshiped on this mountain," the woman said, "but you Jews claim that the place where we must worship is in Jerusalem" (John 4:20).

This was an abrupt change of subject on the heels of Jesus revealing his knowledge of her unflattering past. Jesus graciously did not press her on her sins, but he responded to her comments on worship with the following, "Believe me, a time is coming when you will worship the Father neither on this mountain nor in Jerusalem....A time is coming and has now come when the true worshipers will worship the Father in Spirit and in truth, for they are the kind of worshipers the

Father seeks" (verses 21-23). It's not important where you worship, in other words, it's important how you worship. The woman was into the details of worship, as many Christians are today. To which Jesus would still say, worship is neither here nor there, because it is everywhere. It is an inner reality. It happens in Spirit and in truth, and because it happens in Spirit and truth, it can take place anywhere, all the time.

Rich Mullins, the late contemporary Christian troubadour, left us an enduring chorus that captures this in song: "Everywhere I Go I See You." How is it that a person can see God everywhere? Is it because God is starting to show up everywhere? Is it because some wealthy Christian took out an ad campaign to put billboards about God all over town? Is it because God has suddenly become the topic of conversation? Is it because September 11, 2001, got everyone thinking about God? Is it because Christians have finally become a presence in politics and thus the news? Is it because Christian football players are caught on television holding hands and praying? Is it because Hollywood has finally given the Christian character more than one dimension? Is it because Jesus is running in an ad campaigning against gas-guzzling SUVs? These are all sightings of a cultural God that may or may not have anything to do with the real Jesus. None of this is what Rich Mullins was talking about.

Rich was talking about sightings of God that were the result of his love for God and his passion for the truth. He saw God everywhere he looked because God was on his mind all the time. He saw God everywhere because he was always worshiping God in Spirit and in truth. Rich saw God everywhere because he figured out a way to pay attention to God and the world at the same time. In fact, he found out that a mind on God is more easily directed at what it was made to do in all areas of life. To borrow the essence of an antidrug ad campaign: This is your mind; this is your mind on God. And these two states are the difference between just existing and worshiping.

We exist to worship. We think; therefore we worship. Unbelievers are a form of worship without knowing it by reflecting the nature of their Creator. Everything that breathes worships by being what it is. Worship is not some new strategy for reaching a postmodern church; it is what we were always meant to do. When praise and worship ceases to be a fad for the church, lovers of God will still be worshiping.

We worship by way of our gifts. We have been given everything we possess. When we use what we have, we are fulfilling the purpose for which we were made. Running was a "high" for Eric Liddell (*Chariots of Fire*) because he felt God's pleasure when he ran. It was his gift. Running, for him, was an act of worship. I am hard-pressed to think of any use of mind and body, with the obvious exception of sinning, that isn't or can't be a similar act of worship.

This is worship that is up to me. It is my idea and my execution. True worship cannot be prompted or coerced. It doesn't happen to me; I make it happen by setting my mind and heart on God. It is that inner desire to love God with everything I do—see God in everything I see.

A Deeper Level

Returning to the story of Jesus at the well of Jacob: When the disciples returned after running into town for some food, they "were surprised to find him talking with a woman. But no one asked, 'What do you want' or 'Why are you talking with her?'" (John 4:27). Instead, they tried to get Jesus to eat something, but he told them he wasn't hungry. "I have food to eat that you know nothing about" (verse 32). The disciples, oblivious to the conversation that had transpired between Jesus and the woman, said to each other, "Could someone have brought him food?" (verse 33).

The scene is almost humorous. Jesus is caught up in the joy and fulfillment of doing his Father's will. He has just watched the life-changing power of his truth and love transform a woman right before his eyes from being a five-time loser to being loved and accepted by someone who knows everything about her—everything she's trying to forget but can't. Ignoring the disciples, Jesus looks out on the fields and sees the woman—you could call her the first evangelist—bringing the whole town out to meet him, their turbans gleaming in the sun like a field white with harvest. "Open your eyes and look to the fields!" (verse 35). Jesus is actually worshiping his Father here, feeding on the joy of doing his will and feeling a deep compassion for so many who are lost. He is so taken up with the Father's purposes in the world that temporal things pale in comparison. He will eat eventually, and that will be worship too, but right now there are other matters of greater concern.

The pathetic disciples are watching the same thing and can't see past their noses. They are focused on their own petty embarrassment and judgment over finding Jesus alone with a woman, and they are worrying about his next meal. They are looking on the surface of things; Jesus is looking deeper, where the will of God the Father is revealed, and he is worshiping.

People in the world are dying all around us without Christ, and much of the church is caught up and worried about what to do with a worship service that is not the beginning and the end of worship anyway. Everyone seems to be grasping onto their own little piece of worship as if that is all there is. Believe me, there is plenty of worship to go around. There is a whole life of it for anyone who wants it.

Thirty years ago a revival swept across this country that came to be known as the Jesus Movement. Thousands of young people were coming to Christ, and many of them made their way into the church. It happened so fast and in such great numbers that churches forgot to tell these kids to cut their hair, change into suits, and leave their guitars outside. That meant that the churches that opened their doors to this influx had their "worship" drastically altered. The joy and reality of new life brought its own vitality. Churches were looking out instead of in, and they were nourished on food that the old church knew nothing about. New life and a deeper understanding of worship changed the way they saw everything.

Every Little Thing

Worship, then, is not something we do only in church as much as it is a way of doing everything we do. "And whatever you do, whether in word or deed, do it all in the name of the Lord Jesus, giving thanks to God the Father through him" (Colossians 3:17).

In his spiritual classic, *Practicing the Presence of God*, Brother Lawrence found God in the kitchen of a monastery when he decided to perform his mundane duties there in the name of the Lord. People all over the world are still benefiting from what he found in that kitchen. God desires to enter into all our activities and enable us to see him in them, but he requires an invitation, or at least an effort to be aware of him. God's eyes are always on us. Is there any reason why ours can't be on him?

I am convinced we are rarely ever conscious of the true significance of our lives, down to their slightest detail. Something else is going on here than what meets the eye. We are not merely marking time. We are engaged in warfare, we are spreading good news, we are a fragrance of Christ, we are always being led, we are constantly on display as the church to powers and forces unknown to us. In Ephesians, Paul explains what he calls the "administration of this mystery, which for ages past was kept hidden in God, who created all things. His intent was that now, through the church, the manifold wisdom of God should be made known to the rulers and authorities in heavenly realms" (Ephesians 3:9-10).

I take this to mean that something bigger than our daily existence is at stake here on earth. Certainly God's eye doesn't miss anything, but he may not be the only one watching. I believe this verse speaks of an otherworldly significance to our daily lives that may make our choices more crucial than we could ever imagine. What God is doing with us (which includes what we do without even knowing it) is establishing some of his wisdom somewhere in the universe. Admittedly, there is some speculation here on my part, but I am confident of this: We will find out in heaven that our daily lives were far more significant than we ever realized on earth. Part of learning to worship God all the time is understanding this by faith and beginning to act as if our daily lives made a difference.

Flight 468

What would this look like? Mostly it is an acknowledgement of God's presence and purposes in the ordinary things around us. I'm flying in an airplane right now as I write this. Whenever I think of the tonnage of one of these flying machines actually lifting off the ground and hurtling through the air at 550 mph I am amazed at what God has enabled human beings to do. There is a movie playing on the little screen in the row in front of me. I don't have earphones, but it is a futuristic film starring kids with amazing computer gadgets, appliances, and modes of travel. Without any understanding of what is going on, I can marvel at the high level of imagination displayed. Somebody's mind has been working overtime on this one. I reflect on how imagination is one of God's gifts to us as men and women in his image. Someone has created another world in this film and spliced it together so that we can visit it for a couple of hours, which makes me realize how much more remarkable is the real world we are living in and the stories we are making that are all a part of God's mastermind. Only our world is real, it is unfolding in a dynamic universe every minute and more than swallows up the imaginary one on the little screen.

Then I look at the people around me, every person beautiful in his or her own way. I think of God fashioning them, knowing who they are from the beginning of time. I think of the complexity of each of their lives, and I wonder how God will fit into their stories. I can choose to pray for them and know it will make a difference. Perhaps some of them don't have anyone to pray for them right now. I notice the man two seats over is reading *The New Revelation: A Conversation with God,* and I remember what Paul said in his message to the Greek philosophers in Athens:

> The God who made the world and everything in it is the Lord of heaven and earth and does not live in temples built by hands. And he is not served by human hands, as if he needed anything. Rather, he himself gives everyone life and breath and everything else. From one man he made all the nations, that they should inhabit the whole earth, and he marked out their appointed times in history and the boundaries of their lands. God did this so that they would seek him and perhaps reach out for him and find him, though he is not far from any one of us. "For in him we live and move and have our being." As some of your own poets have said, "We are his offspring" (Acts 17:24-28).

The man reading the book is exemplifying this very thing. He is seeking for God, and perhaps reaching out and finding him. But the irony, as Paul points out, is that while he is searching for God, God is all over him, breathing down his neck—more than that—God is in every breath he takes.

Then I think of myself sitting here, a myriad of synapses and chemical reactions keeping me alive, none of which I am aware of. A human biologist could explain much of this to me, but what is most amazing is that all of this physical matter contains me—a personality, a soul and spirit in the image of my Creator who died so that I might live on, beyond the confines of this physical existence and this plane.

All of this is worthy of my worship, and, in fact, it has been an act of worship merely to think about these things, meditate on them, and write them down. All I did was perceive my position here on this plane at a level below the surface. There I found much to worship God about. It seems as though it could just go on and on.

And it does.

TEN

Whatever Is True...

...think about such things.

PHILIPPIANS 4:8

What do you think about when you're not aware of what you're thinking? An argument could be made that a person's thoughts are their own business. This is true to a point, but sooner or later a person's thoughts become the business of everyone around them. That's because a person's thoughts never stay their thoughts. Eventually their thoughts determine their actions—more than that—they determine who they are.

Jesus put it this way: "The good man brings good things out of the good stored up in his heart, and the evil man brings evil things out of the evil stored up in his heart. For out of the overflow of the heart his mouth speaks" (Luke 6:45 NIV). When this overflow takes place, we don't know. A person may be able to live something that is contrary to their heart for a while (for example, the Pharisees), but sooner or later his inner life becomes his outer expression, good or bad.

Many Scriptures place a high value on what we think about, but none as clearly as Paul's admonition in Philippians: "Finally, brothers and sisters, whatever is true, whatever is noble, whatever is right, whatever is pure, whatever is lovely, whatever is admirable—if anything is excellent or praise-worthy—think about such things" (Philippians 4:8).

135

This verse immediately raises the question as to how one does this. Are we to arrange our world and our experiences so as to only encounter that which is true, noble, right, pure, lovely, admirable, and worthy of praise so that these will be the things that fill our minds most of the time? Though this appears to be the most popular interpretation of this verse, it is hard to imagine anyone really finding and maintaining such a pristine environment for any length of time. Our environment and responsibilities in society force us to encounter much that is false, ignoble, wrong, impure, ugly, less than admirable, and not worthy of praise. If this is the way this verse is to be interpreted, we are once again talking about a sort of culture war for believers. How can we limit being exposed to bad things if we are to be in the world? Can we realistically ensure only good things will enter our minds?

The important distinction to make here is that Paul is not talking about what we are exposed to—what we encounter in the world—but rather, what we think about. What we see and what we think about are two very different things. This is not about what is in our field of vision as much as it is about what occupies our mind.

I believe the intended application of this text is quite different from its more popular use in evangelical circles as a proof text for a blanket rejection of culture. It was meant to be more of a guide for carrying on a spiritual life in the real world. To the extent that one is going to engage culture, this is how to determine the "take away" value of the experience. This would have direct application to our level of participation in popular media such as television, film, print, and Internet use. Rarely will we encounter anything in this realm that is completely clean and pure, and we have seen how this can apply to Christian things as well as what is in the mainstream. (Christian things are not safe and free of impurities just because they are "Christian.") But there are few things aside from pornography that don't contain at least something that is true, noble, right, pure, lovely, admirable, or worthy of praise. If we keep our minds focused on finding these things in the world, we will discover a way of redeeming our involvement in it.

Instead of trying to make the world conform to our values, something which has already made many people enemies of the gospel for the wrong reasons, we can find and focus on what we value in the world. I am the one in charge of what I think. I am not a victim or prisoner of my culture. No one is tying me up and forcing me to think anything. Just as I can choose what I want to be exposed to, I can also choose what to look for and think about in relation to what I'm exposed to.

In an Old Testament story, Daniel and his three friends were fully acquainted with the pagan Babylonian culture they were exiled in as well as with the things of the Lord. "To these four young men God gave knowledge and understanding of all kinds of literature and learning….In every matter of wisdom and understanding about which the king questioned them, he found them ten times better than all the magicians and enchanters in his kingdom" (Daniel 1:17-20). They could not have served at such a high level in government without being familiar with all aspects of Babylonian culture, yet they were not corrupted by that culture. They were undoubtedly able to keep their minds focused on that which is true, noble, right, pure, lovely, admirable, and worthy of praise even while serving in Babylon.

Then there is the apostle Paul's example when he was in Athens. While there the Bible says he "looked carefully at [their] objects of worship" and even retrieved something useful for his message to the city's pagan philosophers (Acts 17:23). He found an altar labeled "To an Unknown God" and found this to be true about it: There is a God that they admittedly knew nothing about. He was able to find something true in their culture that was useful to the message of the gospel.

We cannot make the world true, noble, right, pure, lovely, admirable, and worthy of praise, but we can find and celebrate that which is true, noble, right, pure, lovely, admirable, and worthy of praise in the world. And even if we cannot necessarily further these things in our culture, no one can stop us from finding them and thinking on them as much as we choose. "Think about such things," that is what Paul is asking us to do.

But there is another reason we must figure out how to stay focused on what is pleasing to God in a world full of that which is not, and that has to do with the company we keep and why we keep it.

Bad Company

As Christians in the world, we are living among unbelievers. These are our neighbors, teammates, family members, coworkers, and to some extent, though not as much as it could be, our friends. If we were here just to be good people and go to heaven someday, then we would do best to limit our contact with anyone and anything that is not Christian, and given the current decadence of Western culture, a monastery wouldn't be out of the question. But the gospel is about more than personal piety. If we are representatives of Jesus Christ, we are here for more than ourselves.

Piety can be selfish. Self-righteousness is full of self; it puts self above others. It says there are people in the world who are bad for me. I must avoid certain people if I am to maintain my own personal holiness. But if you think about Jesus and how he feels about sinners, this attitude is not holy at all. It is, in fact, what is at the heart of the pride and religious separatism he abhorred.

Ever wonder why we are here on this planet? If the world is so bad for us, why doesn't God rescue us out of it? Why doesn't he rapture us immediately upon our statement of faith? Are we here to live the most sanctimonious lives possible, or are we here to carry the good news of God's forgiveness to those who need it as much as we do? If the answer is affirmative to both of these at the same time (which I believe it is), how do we pull this off? How do we manage to stay holy while still maintaining a real connection to the world around us?

This is where personal morality and the gospel sometimes appear to be at odds. If we are here only to be holy, moral people, then we should stay away from bad company. But if we are also going to be in this world for the sake of representing the gospel, we will have to find out where we can participate and what we can affirm.

Jesus was almost always found in bad company. He spent his time with tax collectors, prostitutes, and common sinners. He was an offense to the religious leaders of the day because he chose to live this way. Yet Jesus compromised nothing of his own holiness because of his friends. He had a kind of resilient piety—a sacred solidness at his core that was unaffected by the evil around him. He did not need to close his eyes to the world. Instead, his eyes were wide open and often filled with tears over the predicament of the people he had compassion for.

Being in the world requires this kind of self-policed inner morality. Spiritual maturity should be the goal of all believers, but a Christianity that requires a person to go through their whole life with cultural blinders on is a Christianity that cannot speak to the age. This is why maintaining an inner standard that can find and celebrate what is worthy of praise is better than demanding the world conform to our requirement of holiness. This would force us away from sinners who need the gospel as much as we do.

How Ready Should We Be?

Over 30 years ago, Larry Norman defined a spiritual movement in this country with a song he intended to leave behind. "I Wish We'd All Been Ready" became the standard for a Jesus movement that swept across North America and parts of the Western world. He was not kidding, nor were we. The song was intended to be left behind after we'd been raptured out of the world into heaven, and now 30 years later, we are the ones left behind and the song has become a big money-making book idea.

It was a concept I bought into in a big way at a very formative period in my life. I took this to believe that I was part of a special generation that would not have to see death. Not only that, I believed I would not have to see adulthood and all the negative aspects of responsibility that go along with being an adult. Somewhere along the line I woke up to the fact I was a card-carrying, mortgage-owning, SUV-driving, insurance-buying, college-funding, retirement-wasting member of a materialistic society. My wife says that when we bought our first house I went into a fetal position and haven't come out of it since.

She's right; I did. I have struggled with much of my life since the Jesus Movement, and most of that struggle is due to the fact that I believe God let me down by not staging the rapture 30 years ago. Of course he didn't let me down—that is only my perception of these events—but it describes my attitude nonetheless. We really did believe it. Hal Lindsay wrote a bestselling book about it. Every day since then that I wake up and find myself still on this planet is a disappointment of sorts. Christ was going to return very soon, and in God's time, that is still true; I just chose to use that fact to excuse myself from growing up. Even as I write this, I am speaking to a large convention of college students on the East Coast. Last night I noticed a contingent of pastor types in suits and ties and wondered what those old guys were doing here. Then I realized they were younger than me. This resistance just won't go away.

This is one of the reasons why I love reminiscing about the Jesus Movement. I know I romanticize it. God moved in mighty ways then, but that does not mean he isn't moving today. It also doesn't mean we were right about everything back then. This overemphasis on the imminent return of Christ was one thing that clouded our vision. In some cases we were so heavenly minded as to not be any earthly good.

The gospel was paramount to the message of the Jesus Movement, but the gospel stopped with a person's soul.

Emphasis on prophecy and the end times often causes Christians to take a dim view of our present situation here on earth. Is our life on earth merely a necessary evil to be endured until that time when we are finally released from this bondage to a sinless life in heaven—heaven, of course, being someplace other than where we are now? Are we just waiting it out down here?

The Kingdom Came

It is in light of these events and trends that I find the parables of Jesus so important. Jesus often spoke in a manner that seemed to contradict a totally otherworldly existence. He often talked as if the kingdom of heaven had already come to earth. He even taught us to ask in our prayers that God's will in heaven would be done on earth. According to Jesus, there is nothing to wait for. Heaven has come to earth, and heaven is now.

Two examples in the words of Jesus put the kingdom of God in present-tense experience. "But if I drive out demons by the finger of God, then the kingdom of God has come to you" (Luke 11:20) and "Once, having been asked by the Pharisees when the kingdom of God would come, Jesus replied, 'The kingdom of God does not come with your careful observation, nor will people say, "Here it is," or "There it is," because the Kingdom of God is within you'" (Luke 17:20-21 NIV).

And then there are numerous parables that begin "The kingdom of heaven is like..." and go on to capture what appears to be very earthly situations with evil present. This is certainly not the heaven I learned about in Sunday school. This kingdom has weeds in with the good wheat (Matthew 13:24-30), leaven in the bread (Matthew 13:33), tiny seeds that grow into bushes the size of a tree (Matthew 13:31-32), and good and bad fish all in the same net (Matthew 13:47-50).

There is no way you can read these stories and not come up with the conclusion that heaven is already here and we have the privilege of operating in it, but that means a huge paradigm shift for many of us. Here are just a few ways we may need to change our thinking:

1. *The kingdom of heaven (at least the one on earth) has evil in it, and it does not appear that our job in the kingdom is damage control.* In both instances of the weeds in with the wheat and the bad fish with the good, nothing is to be done until the final judgment, and then the weeding out process will be performed by God and his angels. This does not mean we don't "test the spirits" of those who teach us (1 John 4:1). There will be false teachers among us as promised. It simply means we will not have a perfect church here on earth.

2. *The kingdom of heaven on earth has to include the presence of evil because I am in it.* I'm the bad apple. It is the ultimate arrogance to let ourselves in and then shut the door on everyone else, as if we deserved to be in the kingdom and they don't. From many of the stories he told, it is clear that Jesus would have us welcoming in all who would come.

3. *In spite of the presence of evil, the kingdom of heaven on earth has great worth to God.* He would sell everything he has to buy it, and indeed, he has done that very thing through the sacrifice of his only Son. We have value even in our imperfection (Romans 5:8).

4. *God still has ownership of this world.* The old hymn "This Is My Father's World" is true. Sometimes we focus so much on the evil in this world and on Satan as the "ruler of the kingdom of the air" (Ephesians 2:2) that we forget that this is still God's world and the devil has only been given limited opportunity to do his evil work. God did not abandon the world when he let evil in. He is still at work here, and his kingdom is doing just fine.

If we can't even talk about the kingdom of heaven on earth without making room for evil in it, then we can't set ourselves aside and be aloof to the world because of the evil there. That would be the ultimate form of hypocrisy, a thing for which Jesus condemned the Pharisees. The same God who can overlook our sin because of the cross is willing to overlook the sins of others as well. We cannot set ourselves apart without treading on the grace of God.

Street People

When Jesus explained the parable of the weeds sown among the good seed, he said of the harvest (the final judgment): "The Son of Man will send out his angels, and they will weed out of his kingdom everything that causes sin and all who do evil" (Matthew 13:41). Notice whose kingdom it is. It's his kingdom. You could say that the world right now is the kingdom of God with evil let in. Take away the evil, and you have heaven on earth.

The privilege we have as believers, then, is to find and operate in this kingdom of heaven on earth. We do not have to be deluded by the ruler of the kingdom of the air. We can be in the world and experience what is good about it. This is not only a privilege, it is a responsibility.

Part of that good is the value Jesus found in every human being. God put his image there. And he seeks that treasure as a treasure hidden in a field (Matthew 13:44). In his joy he bought the whole field even though he was only interested in the treasure in it. We too can seek this hidden treasure in the world. It is the way God loves through us. We also in some way buy into the whole field in order to do this.

Every time we pray the prayer Jesus taught us to pray, we say: "Thy will be done in earth, as it is in heaven" (Matthew 6:10 KJV). I think we implicate ourselves by that prayer. Who is going to do his will on earth if it isn't us? I don't believe he means for us to just stand by and watch. Who is going to get dirty intermingling with sinners and inviting them into the kingdom if it isn't us? Who else is there who cares?

Remember the parable Jesus told about the king throwing a banquet and all the invited guests had other things to do, so he sent his servants out into the streets to bring in whomever they found there? (Matthew 22:1-10). That parable is all about us. The Jewish leaders who rejected Jesus were the invited guests; we're the street people who shouldn't be here. Have we so quickly forgotten the sheer grace that got us in the door? Are we demanding that sinners clean up their act first and then maybe we'll think about letting them in? Have we become the new Pharisees?

To look at sinners and see them the way we want to be seen—through the eyes of our salvation—is to focus on what is true, noble, right, pure, lovely, admirable, and worthy of praise in the world. These are people, made in God's image and beloved by him, who, regardless of what they look like now, for all we know are children of the light. We need to learn to take the bad along with the good, especially in light of the fact that we were accepted that way. To look at people as obnoxious and offensive is to spit into the face of God.

Direct Encounters

One of the saddest things about our modern life in the Western world is that our lives in the cities and the suburbs separate us so much from the impact of God's created world. We live in houses, ride in cars, breathe forced air all day inside of office buildings, and return home to watch a nature show on television. The average American has very little direct contact with the things God made. Most of our lives are surrounded by mediated experiences—something stands between us and the natural creation. For all intents and purposes, most of us live in a man-made world.

This makes it harder to find what is true, noble, right, pure, lovely, admirable, and worthy of praise in our daily life, for all of God's creation, in spite of the fall, shows off every one of these characteristics in abundance. Still, there remain touches of his handiwork that can grace our lives even without taking time to drive into the woods. A tree in autumn, a blanket of snow, a sunset, a thunderstorm, the smell of freshly mown grass, or sunlight through a leaf are direct experiences of God in his creation that are still accessible to most people on an average day. The proverbial "stop and smell the roses" applies here. Sometimes one of these marvelous displays can creep up on us when we least expect it. The point is to stop and worship. Let God's presence touch you through what he has made. Don't just smell the roses, touch them; you are touching what he touched. It's a direct encounter.

I'm working on my laptop right now at the dining room table of my home. The sun is not up yet. At this hour, in this place, there is very little I can experience in the direct natural realm that has not been mediated in some way by human hands. Even the air I breathe has been altered by the house I'm in and the furnace that is blowing it into the room. But there are two things I can experience from God's creation without moving from my chair. One is the sound of the rain hitting the roof and falling into puddles outside—a soothing, steady sound. The other is a vase of cut flowers that sits as a centerpiece on the table: red berries, a few red roses, pine needles, and strands of white orchids. It is Christmastime, and this is a beautiful display of color that God made. But then I realize that God did not create these things all bunched together like this. I would not find this arrangement anywhere in the natural world. They were artfully selected and arranged by my wife, who loves flowers and creates a new bouquet each week. A case could also be made that the light that illuminates these colors right now is artificial. However, I can just imagine what the bouquet will look like when late afternoon sun streams in through the window. So I praise God for what I can see and touch as well as for the knowledge and wisdom he gave to display it in such a way. It occurs to me that this bouquet has been here for six days and I have not noticed or thought about it until now. Look what I've been missing.

The interaction of my wife with the florist who bought the flowers from the grower who grew them points out the artful way in which we interact with God and use the gifts he has given us to be cocreators with him. This opens the whole world of the arts—music, film, dance, drama, writing, sculpture, fine art, design—where we can find a good deal of what is true, noble, right, pure, lovely, admirable, and worthy of praise regardless of the attitude of the participants toward the Creator. Christians have tragically counted God out of much of this realm due to a dualistic world view that required some sort of religious or Christian theme in order for God to be involved. It shouldn't be that hard to figure out that something created by a human being, who in turn was and is being created by God, can express God's glory in some form.

Starry Night

Two Sundays ago our pastor preached in front of a large-screen image of Vincent Van Gogh's famous impressionist rendering *Starry Night*. I am not sure what is known about Van Gogh's faith. I do know he danced around the edges of sanity most of his life. It isn't even a realistic starry night (it doesn't look like one of God's starry nights), and yet it displays the artist's eye on creation. What we see in this painting is what Van Gogh saw in a starry night. It is, admittedly, more disturbed than most of the nights I have ever seen. But is he not entitled to his interpretation of God's work, and didn't God give him that freedom and ability? As I study this painting (or even think about it now; because it is so famous, I can see it in my mind's eye), I find it true (to Van Gogh's outlook on life and his inner character), noble (in its daring boldness), right (in its use of canvas and paint), pure (in its originality), lovely (in its use of color), admirable (in its accomplishment as a standard spanning almost two centuries), and worthy of praise (as the artist reflects the creativity of the Creator in whose image he was made).

Paul told us to think about such things if we can find any of them. I found in a Van Gogh painting a lot to think about.

Perhaps in the same way we can find a lot to think about in sports, entertainment, and recreation. Any who can appreciate these diversions are very fortunate to have the affluence to enjoy them. But they need not be diversions to faith. These things that fill up a significant amount of our time—things we do not normally look upon as being sacred—can be.

So how do you set up the world to be true, noble, right, pure, lovely, admirable, and worthy of praise? Do you create a Christian world, or do you learn to find Christ in the one we have? The noble are the ones who seek, and find, what they are looking for. "But the seed on good soil stands for those with a noble and good heart, who hear the word, retain it, and by persevering produce a crop" (Luke 8:15).

ELEVEN

Faith at Work

Be joyful always; pray continually; give thanks in all
circumstances...

1 THESSALONIANS 5:16-18 NIV

For most average North American adults who care about finding God in the world, the one place they least expect to see him is their workplace. This is where we are most likely to encounter people in the world and the world in people, and Christians who try to keep themselves separate know this is one arena they can do little about. At one point the apostle Paul refers to the "people of this world" as those who are immoral, greedy, swindlers, and idolaters. But he also states that if we were to try and avoid associating with these people, "[we] would have to leave this world" (1 Corinthians 5:9-10). His assumption, of course, is that we can't, insinuating that we might as well get used to being around these kinds of people because, at least for now, the world is our address. This is a point of view not shared by many Christians, however, who would make Paul's assumption look almost worldly. Assuming associations with sinners may be in the Bible, but it's not in the worldview of many cultural Christians.

The workplace is where we are most likely to rub shoulders with people of other faiths or no faith at all. In this environment, Christians are apt to either wear their faith like a badge or bury it so deep inside that it never comes to the surface.

149

God can often be the last thing on a Christian's mind at work, and, in an ethically challenged, stress-related office, he may be the last thing anybody wants to hear about, but the first thing they need. For many Christians the workplace is the least sacred place on the planet—a place more to be endured from the standpoint of faith than a place where a personal faith could actually flourish.

A large part of this dilemma is the same problem we have been addressing all along in this book: It is a perspective problem—a vision deficiency. Once again, we need vision correction in our thinking about the world to be truly effective in the workplace.

A person who cannot see God in anything but Christian things will be the person most likely to wear their faith at work like a badge, if they wear it at all. The badge comes out when witnessing, attending a company Bible study (if such a privilege exists), or when trying to stand on a higher moral ground than everyone else. But this person sees God only in the badge, and most of the time that badge is in the pocket. So God only gets brought up when he is brought out and pinned to one's shirt. But for the faint glow in this person's pocket, all else is dark. No wonder some Christians do not look forward to going to work.

Once again, the correction to this situation is a different way of thinking—not to be more Christian at work (that is, wear the badge more often) but to see God there to a greater degree. The person who is able to find God in the workplace will end up being more of a Christian without even trying…even without the badge.

Absentmindedly Christian

I grew up on a Christianity that amounted to saying certain things, doing certain things, and not doing other things. It was what I would call a self-conscious Christianity—a Christianity that was calculated and aware of itself. Consequently, it turned into something acted out when the situation called for it, but not at other times, when being a Christian wasn't an issue. It depended on where you were and who you were with. As good evangelical kids, we learned to act one way at church and another way at school.

Then there is another kind of Christianity—a faith that goes along with a person because it is an integral part of who they are—a part of the insides of that person, their heart and mind, their will and emotions. This is a faith that can come out anywhere, anytime, and the owner of this faith is quite absentminded about it. Not that they are forgetful about their faith as much as they forget to try. They don't have to try because their faith is self-evident in their heart.

With the burden of proof resting solely on an external badge of identification, one can see how Christians at work can easily become self-conscious about their faith. "When do I bring God up? Am I making a proper stand for my faith? Do I have the words that would remove all doubt as to whether I am a Christian?" It's a subtle shift to being more concerned about the label than the heart or even the message.

In promotion of one of their albums, Matt Odmark of Jars of Clay, a Christian rock group that has enjoyed some measure of success outside the Christian market, made the comment, "I hope you hear music that is because of faith rather than about it."[1] "Because of" faith is closer to the real thing. It is a view of all of life that grows out of one's faith as a motivating factor in their life. It is a faith that comes from the inside and works its way out. "About it" faith is just words and information. It is conveyed by the cultural Christian badge.

If our faith is something we have to wear or announce or carry by association, it will not be in us as an integral part of our motivation for living. It will be more of a self-conscious faith—aware of itself, aware of defending itself, emanating from the badge, and overly fixated on who wears it and who doesn't. An absentminded faith is self-evident, and it does not have to be called up. Those who are absentmindedly Christian forget what they are supposed to be because they are too busy being who they are.

Curtain Call

At this point it would be good to recall our discussion on worldview in chapter 4 where one worldview had a hard time finding God outside anything that was not clearly Christian. The other found God everywhere. One had an invisible curtain separating the Christian from the secular, the other saw all of life as sacred—no curtain. Those who live with a curtain in their worldview usually go through it on the way to work and stay there until their commute home, maintaining two different personas on either side of it. Those with no curtain in their worldview find that the workplace can be as holy as being at church.

If we have been redeemed by the blood of Christ, we have an opportunity—indeed an obligation—to redeem our place in life as well. This is one of the greatest privileges of being a Christian—to redeem our experience in the world, not just wait to go to heaven and somehow endure a fallen world until we get there.

If, as we have seen already, God came to a material world, then we can have a material faith. We can reclaim what is right about the human experience. This was a part of Christ's task when he was here, and something I believe he intends for us to complete. This is a part of why he saved us, that wherever we are, we might display through our lives something of what God intended us to be. Or as we pray so often: his will in heaven, lived out on earth.

Redeeming the Curse

Work is one of our greatest challenges when it comes to redeeming the human experience, for it was the curse placed on Adam after he ate of the forbidden fruit in the Garden of Eden.

> Cursed is the ground because of you; through painful toil you will eat of it all the days of your life. It will produce thorns and thistles for you,

and you will eat of the plants of the field. By the
sweat of your brow you will eat your food until
you return to the ground, since from it you were
taken (Genesis 3:17-19).

This is surely not a very flattering picture of work. Still,
humanly speaking, it is true, as the experience of most of us
would bear out. But if the curse of the serpent who bruised
the heel of Christ can be overcome by that same Christ who
from the cross delivered a much more telling blow to the evil
one's head (Genesis 3:15), then the precedent has been set for
overcoming this curse as well. Can cursed ground be turned
into something sacred? Can it yield more than thorns and
thistles? Can work itself be redeemed? If it is possible for the
believer to do everything to the glory of God—to pray
without ceasing and rejoice always—then it would appear
that no time or place is beyond reach of the glory and presence of God.

If the curse of work can be redeemed (and I believe it
can), then the first place to reflect its redemption would be
the quality of the work itself. From blue collar to white, from
assembly line to CEO, Christians should be the best there is
in the field in which they work.

It all flows together—our life with God and our life in the
world. You can't separate one from the other. You can't do a
lousy job at work and represent Christ, or at least if you do,
you give him a bad name. You can't be a passionate Christian
and a slacker at work. A passionate Christian is impassioned
about everything they do. You can't love God and mope
around the office. This is the unfortunate thing about a dualistic worldview—it allows you to live two lives in two different realms. A whole Christian lives a whole Christian life
and is never off duty.

I am reminded of a Christmas a few years ago when I
had a most unusual invitation. I received a call earlier that
year from two brothers who own a company in Nebraska
that makes generator-run lights for construction sites and

roadwork. They wanted me to come sing for a company Christmas banquet they put on every year for all of their employees and their families. For this event they pretty much take over a local Ramada Inn and put everyone up for a night so they can enjoy a little getaway for the holidays. In the middle of rural Nebraska in the middle of winter, an indoor pool and a sit-down dinner is a big deal.

It is no secret that these brothers are Christians, but they don't run a Christian business. They just happen to be Christians who run their business as if God were looking over their shoulder watching every move (and, of course, he is). Many of their employees are not Christians, and for that reason they instructed me not to preach in my presentation, but to tell the true story of Christmas all the same. They use the influence of their position to help care for the whole person. If one of their employees is troubled to the point of affecting his work, they don't just fire him, they counsel the person and the family, if necessary. They are committed as much as they can to a quality of life for everyone in the company from the least to the greatest. They are a model of Christians seeing their work as a sacred charge.

It's How You Play the Game

You've heard it said: "It's not whether you win or lose that counts; it's how you play the game." Well, I think that statement applies to more than sports. It can apply to everything we do, especially our witness in the world.

In the late 1970s, the Baltimore Orioles had an outfielder named Pat Kelly, who was a very vocal born-again Christian. According to the Baltimore fan who told me this story, he was a really nice guy, a pretty good hitter, and a terrible fielder. Once, after Kelly had somehow managed to have two balls deflect off his glove and over the fence for home runs for the opposing team, Jim Palmer, the Hall of Fame pitcher who had to absorb those two misplays as a ding in his loss column, ruminated that Kelly would have a much greater impact if he stopped talking about the Bible so much and learned to play the outfield better.

Now I know nothing about the abilities of Pat Kelly or whether he was a guy who played up to his potential or not, but this story is a good example of the need to place importance not only on one's faith but on one's work as well. A big part of our witness is not our witnessing, it's how we play the game: how we live, how we operate, and the character that faith, hard work, and determination develop in our lives.

For some time now, Christians have attempted to witness to the world by being smiling, happy people—really nice guys. We have had a tendency to rely on external identifications to make our faith statement, such as a fish on a business card, a button on our shirt, a sticker on a bumper, a cross around the neck. Or perhaps it's the things we don't do that are supposed to make us stick out in the world as different, something that in itself is supposed to carry its own weight as a witness. I have heard serious testimonies where the statement "No thanks, I don't drink" is tantamount to effectively sharing the gospel at an office party.

But like Jim Palmer's remark, it's sometimes more important that a Christian catch the ball than talk about Jesus. Not that we shouldn't be talking about Jesus; it just makes a big difference who's doing the talking.

Our life on earth need not be at odds with our place in heaven. How we play the game is not less important than, or separate from, our relationship to God. They really should be one and the same. Our walk *is* our witness; our life *is* our testimony. A Christian baseball player doesn't pray and then go out and play baseball. He prays and plays at the same time. For Pat Kelly, concentrating on the catch, in other words, was as important as giving the testimony. These things are not, and should not be, exclusive of each other.

Jim Palmer's statement indicates that, at least in his opinion, Kelly's commitment to Christ took something off his play on the field, as if his concentration on God made him lose concentration on the ball. I have a feeling, if that was the case, then God would rather have had him catch the ball too. (I happen to think God's a big baseball fan anyway.)

Concentration on God should mean concentration on our job, our work, even our play and recreation. It is not a choice of one over the other. If we understand the first one correctly (our relationship with God), there will be a way in which God joins us in whatever we are doing. This is essential to a good Christian worldview.

If Pat Kelly had led a Bible study for some of his teammates before the game, would that have been a much bigger deal to God than how he handled a catchable ball in the outfield? I don't think so. God is interested as much in our play, our work, our rest, our rising up, and our lying down as he is in our praying, our study of the Bible, our church attendance, or our witness in the world. If Christ is in us by his Holy Spirit as Paul teaches (1 Corinthians 6:19), then God is in some marvelously unseen way participating in everything we do. God is on the field. He is in the office. He is in the car, and everywhere we are.

Or Maybe It's How You Kick the Ball

My DC area amateur sports commentator—the one who shared with me the story on Pat Kelly—recently sent me another story that is worth including here.

Our local sports talk radio station devotes the bulk of its evening drive-time show to the Washington Redskins. The Redskins lost their kicker to a season-ending injury and signed a replacement who is evidently a Christian. He has never kicked in the NFL before, and his college statistics are less than imposing. The two gentlemen who host the show were talking with a "beat" reporter who covers the team. It went something like this:

Host 1: "I understand the new kicker is also a minister?"

Reporter (with more than a trace of sarcasm): "Yes, and he will definitely tell you about it."

Host 1: "I've heard that if he doesn't make it as a kicker, his plan is to become a pastor?"

Host 2: "Well, if he kicks poorly, a whole lot of fans will be screaming for Jesus!"

Contrast this with Darrell Green, in his twentieth (and final) season with the Redskins. At age 41, he is somehow still able to play cornerback, often covering men half his age. He is universally respected and loved by the DC community because, in addition to performing at a high level, he spends his free time working with charities and giving back to the community. When his starting job was literally handed to Deion Sanders, he could have lashed out at the coach or sulked, but instead he publicly supported the decision and said he wanted what was best for the team.

Once a week, he appears on this same radio station with these same hosts. They often attempt to involve him in some crass joke or controversy. I have been amazed at how deftly and gracefully he handles himself. Never condemning, never "ducking" an issue, he always responds with honesty, charm, humor, and grace without being overly critical. The hosts love having him on their show. His performance and character have earned him the right to be heard, so that when he does speak about spiritual things, they respect him.

This is in keeping with how we all could be carrying ourselves in our jobs, and in all our relationships with unchurched people, for that matter. This is a testimony as to our lives lived out with character, excellence, and even a bit of flare. It is a truer measure of the reality of one's faith for others to uncover it while coming to us for something else—and would that we had something else to interest them.

No Need to Justify

This is reason enough for us as Christians to be interesting, knowledgeable people to be around. I often hear Christians needing to justify their involvement in secular activities or pursuits. It might be a golf game or an obsession with model railroads or a penchant for mystery novels. These need not be things that leave God out. When you think about it, no one can ever shut God out of anything; we simply choose to not include him in our thinking. If we do, this is to our disadvantage. He didn't leave; we just shut him out of our minds.

The other day a pastor I was with apologized for his lovely home in the mountains. He had to tell me how the property had been inherited and how some of the labor was a gift from skilled members of his congregation. I looked at the mountain view the house commanded and the beauty of its construction and told him there was no need to apologize. I imagined God enjoyed his home as much as he did.

I was elated the day I discovered that God was having as much fun at a Minnesota Twins/Texas Rangers ball game as I was. I made this discovery when I realized how much truth I could find illustrated by what was going on down on the field. (Remember focusing on the praiseworthiness of all we do as discussed in the last chapter.) When we finally get this straightened out, we will see the world and our activity in it from a single-minded perspective. There are no longer Christian and secular things or activities. All of life is God's.

Our witness, then, is not something we turn on and off— a badge we pull out on certain occasions. It's something that is going on all the time, and everything we do reflects it and is important to it. A commendable job at whatever we do commends our witness. Jim Palmer was right; Mr. Kelly needed to work on his fielding.

As Christians, we need to focus on our work in the world and not think that our relationship with God is compromised by it. Our witness and our work cohabit the same temple, and God can be praised in both.

On another occasion, I am told that Pat Kelly told Earl Weaver, the then-feisty manager of the Baltimore team, that he should try to "walk with the Lord more," to which Weaver responded, "I'd rather walk with the bases loaded." In either case, our walk is everything.

TWELVE

Christ and the Ordinary

I praise you, Father, Lord of heaven and earth, because you have hidden these things from the wise and learned, and revealed them to little children. Yes, Father, for this was your good pleasure.

LUKE 10:21

Jesus began his ministry where we would least expect him to, at a wedding, doing what we would least expect him to be doing, making good wine—barrels of it. Not just any wine, mind you...good wine. Instant vintage. All those acids and tannins in perfect equilibrium. Something that only old vines, a good winemaker, and lots of time can create. I've always been more than a little curious about how this first miracle went down.

> On the third day a wedding took place at Cana in Galilee. Jesus' mother was there, and Jesus and his disciples had also been invited to the wedding. When the wine was gone, Jesus' mother said to him, "They have no more wine."
>
> "Dear woman, why do you involve me?" Jesus replied. "My time has not yet come."
>
> His mother said to the servants, "Do whatever he tells you" (John 2:1-5).

161

Doesn't there appear to be something missing here between Jesus' rebuff and Mary's directive? Any other mother making a comment to her son about the wine running out would not carry with it any implication beyond the fact that maybe it was time to go home. But her comment clearly implied Christ's involvement in some other way—as if they both knew he could do something about this particular problem, and Mary chose to override him. Either Mary had an inside track on this as the first public miracle of Jesus, or she and Joseph had already benefited from his fine art of wine making at home and she felt it would be a nice gesture. Equally strange is the fact that Jesus decides to defer to her and perform the miracle anyway. It's hard to know what to make of all this.

To be sure, there is plenty of symbolism in this act. There is the wine that will become very important at the end of Christ's ministry, or the "third day" that begins this story that foreshadows Christ's death and resurrection, or the celebration of the event as a beginning of his ministry, or the symbol of Christ and the church as his bride, or the miracle of the transformation itself of water to wine, but for me, the biggest significance of this first miracle is how *insignificant* it was. No one was healed, no one was raised from the dead, no demons were cast out, no hungry people were fed. It wasn't even necessary. Jesus and Mary were invited guests. It wasn't their responsibility to provide wine. At any other party, it would have meant the party was over; time to go home. Why this? Why now?

The very fact that this miracle defies reason is what makes it so extraordinary. It's even a miracle of excess. Wasn't it the master of the banquet who commented to the bridegroom how "everyone brings out the choice wine first and then the cheaper wine after the guests have had too much to drink" (verse 10) implying, of course, that they had already reached the point in the evening beyond which anyone could tell the difference?

Evangelicals have always struggled over interpreting this first miracle. Not only is Jesus providing alcohol at a party, something that is forbidden in most Christian circles, but he is providing it after people have already had too much to drink! How do you dance around this? This is an offense to our best sensibilities. Even the old Baptist argument that wine in New Testament times was more like our grape juice breaks down here. How could too much grape juice impair one's judgment? We're talking about a party where the host alludes to some who have already had enough to drink, and Jesus supplies more. It would make more sense to most Christians for Jesus to be doing the opposite thing here— turning their wine into water and shutting down their par-tying. No evangelical would have problems with that kind of action. But this water-to-wine thing (six water jars each holding 20 to 30 gallons!) is scandalous to our best sense of judgment. If it was anybody other than Jesus doing this, it would not be interpreted as a "miracle." It would more likely be looked upon as something evil or sinister.

I am not going to attempt any other interpretation of this than the fact that God was entering into and affirming the average, everyday lives of common people and adding his celebration to theirs. Does this miracle somehow sanction people getting drunk? Of course not, especially when the Scriptures clearly admonish against drunkenness. However, I believe it does mean at least two things: 1) God enters the less-than-perfect world of average people and 2) with Jesus, nothing in life is insignificant. Everything is meaningful to a life of faith. Jesus' first miracle kept a party going. How scandalous is that? And yet how life-affirming. How ordinary. How non-religious. This act is an announcement of the fact that the sacred has now touched the commonplace and nothing is the same anymore.

Holy Soldier

> When Jesus had entered Capernaum, a centurion came to him, asking for help.
>
> Lord," he said, "my servant lies at home paralyzed, suffering terribly."
>
> Jesus said to him, "Shall I come and heal him?"
>
> The centurion replied, "Lord, I do not deserve to have you come under my roof. But just say the word, and my servant will be healed. For I myself am a man under authority, with soldiers under me. I tell this one, 'Go,' and he goes; and that one, 'Come,' and he comes. I say to my servant, 'Do this,' and he does it" (Matthew 8:5-9).

Here is a centurion—an officer in the Roman army—who understands something about Jesus based on his own role in the military. Jesus is amazed by this and commends him. "Truly I tell you, I have not found anyone in Israel with such great faith" (verse 10). Not only is this man showing great faith, he is showing his ability to relate God to aspects of his own life experience. He is connecting faith to his work and seeing it in spiritual terms. Who knows what other spiritual implications he could pull from his life because he is thinking this way? Once you start down this path, it becomes easier to find God, and truths about God, in the ordinary, daily responsibilities of our lives.

This should raise corresponding questions in our minds as to similar connections between our vocations and our understanding of God. Questions like: "What is it about my own work experience that might help me understand something in the spiritual realm of life?" Jesus is not only commending the centurion, he is acknowledging that connections like this can and should be made.

One of the more successful business books to be published in recent years (1996) was entitled *Jesus, CEO: Using Ancient Wisdom for Visionary Leadership* by Laurie Beth Jones. Here we have an author and motivational speaker who has found a book's worth of correlations between the life and teachings of Jesus and how to successfully manage people. We should not be surprised when these connections are made, but we are nonetheless. Some might even be offended by this, thinking it blasphemous to imply that Jesus would inspire a good business leadership seminar. Those who would be offended by this are those who like to keep their worlds separate. They feel that to bring Jesus into the business world would somehow muddy his reputation. Such a person must feel pretty dirty themselves about what they do in the world. It does not have to be this way.

It should come as no surprise that this book was not published by a Christian publisher, nor was it marketed in Christian circles, even though it is based on the life of Christ. This is indicative of how prevalent this separatist thinking is among Christians. It passed right under the radar of the subculture and went out to the world (which is actually a good thing when you consider how many books would be helpful outside the Christian subculture but stay trapped there). Laurie Beth Jones went on to publish another book in 2002, *Jesus, Entrepreneur: Using Ancient Wisdom to Launch and Live Your Dreams*. In this book she coins a new word, "spiritreneur," to help describe what she hopes will be a new kind of businessperson desiring to contribute something more to society than just their own success. Wouldn't it benefit the workplace as a whole to have more businesses looking to Jesus for their management style?

A Roman officer made some conclusions about Jesus based on his own work experience and Jesus commended him. This opens up some more avenues of thinking for us as well.

Everyday People

Shortly after this, the Gospel of Matthew tells us that Jesus called "a man named Matthew" while he was sitting at a tax collector's booth (Matthew 9:9). This calling was immediately followed by a dinner at Matthew's house at which a number of other tax collectors and "sinners" were present. The Pharisees and teachers of the Jewish law saw this as heretical. Jesus saw it as an announcement of who would accept him and whom he would accept. The traditional sacred/secular line was not only being crossed, it was being obliterated. This is what upset the Pharisees the most about Jesus. He was removing the distinction by which they separated the sacred from the profane and themselves from everyone else. The Pharisees kept the holy things in the temple. Jesus found the holy in places least expected—at a tax collector's dinner party and in a soldier's faith.

This calling was repeated 11 other times as each of Christ's disciples was selected from various walks of life, but none were from any religious profession. Peter was called while he was fishing. The miraculous, for him, was put in terms of fish in his net—more fish than he could handle. And at the end of three years, when Peter is brought back into relationship with the risen Christ after denying him three times, it is another full net that does the trick. Peter knew it was no stranger instructing him from the shore. It was Jesus. And unable to wait for the boat with all that fish to make it there, he jumped in and swam to his Lord and a campfire breakfast.

Mostly fishermen, ordinary folk, God chose everyday people to make up his most important team. The religious leaders of the day would have seen these individuals as "secular" people, and yet God chose to establish his church through them. God wanted to remove any vestige of "religiosity" from his first followers, indicating his desire to make the gospel relevant to all people and all walks of life. Once again, God comes down and relates to us at the level of our daily lives.

Beauty Among the Ashes

Jesus was constantly sanctioning ordinary life by the way he lived and the stories he told. He was always using common things as illustrations of spiritual truth—things like fields, seeds, fig trees, vines, vineyards, towers, stones, swords, birds, lamps, barns, houses, villages, money, loans, bread, and grain. Were he here today, I can't imagine him not making reference to cities, skyscrapers, airplanes, computers, major appliances, sports equipment, malls, television, film, newspapers, and the Internet. Jesus in the city would not talk about vineyards and farmers because no one would know what he was talking about. But I can imagine him referencing skateboards, sneakers, basketball, clothing styles, boom boxes, and rap music in his stories. He would pick up on what was common to people's lives and the things that make up who we are. In doing so, he would also be showing us that truth is everywhere if we are prepared to look for it.

Life, even in our postmodern world, abides by certain principles that God has built into the universe. Regardless of how we alter the landscape, these truths are still there, and, as our forefathers have said, they are self-evident, though it usually takes someone with better eyesight than us to point them out. This is why we have prophets. This is why we have Jesus.

And then there were the people in his stories—people from all walks of life and none of them religious: farmers, merchants, managers, shepherds, landowners, cooks, fishermen, kings, servants, soldiers, builders, prostitutes, children, bridegrooms, and virgins. These were the people who populated the stories of Jesus and made up his relationships. Out of their lives he drew spiritual significance and by this, I believe, he was implicating that we can do the same.

His first official convert was a Samaritan woman who then brought her whole village out to hear him and many believed. Samaritans were "dogs" to the Jewish leadership. It would be equivalent to what a tattooed, dreadlocked, bones-in-the-nose crowd would seem like to good, upstanding church folk. Who made up Jesus' entourage if it wasn't the lame, the blind, the leprous, and the demon-possessed? Jesus came and preached the gospel to the poor and forever scandalized religion. He mixed up the apple cart. He found treasure in a field and beauty among the ashes. He fed people lunch. He prayed over a little bread and a couple fish and filled the bellies of thousands. There's no way you can truly encounter Jesus and call anything secular anymore. He touched our human lives at every level and found them holy.

Fig Trees and Other Roadside Lessons

> The next day as they were leaving Bethany, Jesus was hungry. Seeing in the distance a fig tree in leaf, he went to find out if it had any fruit. When he reached it, he found nothing but leaves, because it was not the season for figs. Then he said to the tree, "May no one ever eat fruit from you again." And the disciples heard him say it (Mark 11:12-14).

They were just passing by. The day before, Jesus had made his triumphal entry into Jerusalem, where, on a donkey, he was hailed as a king. He and his disciples were returning the next day to Jerusalem after spending the night in nearby Bethany when they passed by the fig tree Jesus singled out for reasons only he knew. The following morning they passed by the same way, for they were staying in Bethany and walking to and from Jerusalem, a sort of commute by foot. This time Peter happened to notice the same fig tree from the day before. "Rabbi, look! The fig tree you cursed has withered!" (Mark

11:21). Jesus then used this as an opportunity to teach his disciples about faith, including the remarkable possibility of telling the nearby mountain to throw itself into the sea and having it be so if they had even a tiny bit of faith to believe it.

I have a hunch this was no unusual occurrence for the disciples. Those teachings about vines and vineyards, sheep and shepherds, seeds and sowers, roads and travelers, wheat fields and harvesters undoubtedly came from similar object lessons from the Galilean countryside they traversed so often. Jesus was constantly teaching from the world around him. God has so ordered his universe that this can be done. The truth about the way things are is evident, so that true truth is never far away. This leaves the possibility open to us to do the same—to not only be taught truth from the world around us, but to find it, and even interact with it as Jesus did with the fig tree. Jesus was not teaching something that was contrary to reality. He was connecting with what his Father made and using it for spiritual purposes. He was always finding the deeper message—the meaning behind things.

One of the most famous walks of Jesus was on the road to Emmaus, a village about seven miles from Jerusalem. It happened that after his resurrection, he appeared to two of his followers as they were walking along this road and trying to make sense of the confusing events of the previous few days during which Jesus had been arrested and crucified. On top of this, there were even rumors of his resurrection. What were they to make of all this? How ironic that Jesus himself would show up to discuss these things with them?

For seven miles a man walked along the road with them "and beginning with Moses and all the Prophets, he explained to them what was said in all the Scriptures concerning himself" (Luke 24:27). The two men were somehow prevented by God from recognizing Jesus as their new traveling companion. Doesn't it make you wonder what they thought of him? Who did they think he was, and why did God blind them to his true identity until the conclusion of their time together? Maybe it was because he wanted their discovery to not be overpowered by the miraculous. Jesus would not always be with them, but the truth of who he was would. Besides, they might not have listened had they known who they were walking with and talking to. They might not have finished their walk. Perhaps God wanted them to have an ordinary experience on an ordinary walk with an ordinary person so the truth would have a greater impact. Had they known who this person was, the ordinary nature of these events might have been overshadowed by the extraordinary, and the long-term effect of the lesson would have been lost. As it was, they walked and talked with a perfect stranger who slowly opened their eyes to the truth. It could have been anyone. It happened to be Jesus.

Holy and Common

There is no greater argument for the sanctity of everyday life than the fact that Jesus made sacraments of ordinary things. Baptizing in a river, washing dirty feet, and turning wine and bread into his body and blood—these are undeniable sanctions of our human experience and proof that anything can be touched by God and made sacred. When these things are removed from their normal settings and made "holy" by association with religious orders, be it robes or vestments or utensils that would not be found in our possession, something of the original intent is lost.

The institutional church has always tried to monopolize the sacraments as a way of making people dependent upon the church and its leaders, and as a way of securing the church's necessity in people's lives. Though evangelicals have always been critical of the Roman Catholic church for these kinds of abuses, we are not without similar guilt. Our "priests" may be called "pastors," but their spirituality may be equally distant from most of us, placing themselves between us and God as a necessary interpreter of God's Word and will. We may not call our water "holy" but it is special water nonetheless, set aside from any other body of water by its placement in the baptismal tank in a predominant place in the front of the church. Our pastors may not speak in Latin, but they speak a language all their own with an air about it that makes them the only ones who possess this lofty lingo. Our communion may not have all the bells and whistles of a Catholic Mass, but the goblets and the dishes and the way the elements are handled create the same effect. We must come to the church for this. We cannot do this without professionals.

I choose to believe that at any given meal, should I decide as head of my household to stop everything and point out to my family the body and blood of Jesus as represented by the bread and wine on the table, that I am not only free to do this, but encouraged by the Lord himself to do so. I do not have to wait for the sanctioned elements of the church and the holy officials there to distribute this meal to me and my family on the first Sunday of the month. The sacraments were purposely made to be ordinary things so that we could continually experience God in the common activity of life. We worship as we go; we do not stop and go somewhere else to worship. We have even made too much of the church building as the "house of God." There were no such houses in the early church; there was just "my place or yours." Both Old and New Testaments are clear about this—the only building on earth suitable to house God is the body of a human being.

Jesus could have chosen sacraments that were foreign to our average existence—things accessible only to professional priests and holy men, but he did not. And what have we done by doing the very thing he refused to do—making these things more holy than they were intended to be? We have once again set the holy aside and doomed most of our existence to the secular. And so we come, Catholic and Protestant alike, to the holy place to get cleansed from the dirt of our daily lives, when our daily lives were designed to be in the holy place at all times.

Come and Have Breakfast

"I'm going fishing" (John 21:1-14).

It was Simon Peter's solution to the confusion and the humiliation of those last days in the life of Christ. The confusion was Christ's death and resurrection, the reality of which the disciples were not able to immediately assimilate, even after seeing him alive. The humiliation was Peter's own denial and his utter sense of failure. His decision to go fishing was as much a reverting to his old ways of running away from a problem as anything. *I'm going back to what I know I can do. I've had enough of this discipleship business. I was never the religious type anyway. Leave that to the Pharisees and the Jewish leaders. And even if Jesus is really alive, I'm not worthy to serve him anyway, after what I did. That's just one too many times I've had my foot in my mouth. I'm going back to fishing. At least that's predictable.*

Or so he thought. When Peter got back to shore and found that Jesus had some fine coals burning and fish on the fire, that was when Jesus uttered four important words: "Come and have breakfast." There was so much to say, so much to straighten out, so much to demand, so much to forgive. But first...breakfast.

Why are these words so important? Because they are so ordinary and human. They typify Christ's mission on earth. To invite us to our next meal, to sanction our human experience while showing us what it is all about at the same time. He's even prepared this meal for us. He could have stood on the shore and lectured the disciples. Instead, he made them breakfast. Oh, he had things to say to them all right, but he waited until after they finished eating, and then he said them like he always had, while they walked along the way back to Jerusalem.

THIRTEEN

Joining the Adventure

Micawber's dull life, with its tedious toils,
All at once seemed a hundred times duller,
As he straddled a palette and squeezed out some oils
And discovered the wonders of COLOR![1]

JOHN LITHGOW

Most Americans with any television experience will recognize John Lithgow as High Commander Dick Solomon in the long-running NBC comedy series *3rd Rock from the Sun.* Those who are true fans, however, might know he is also an author of songs and poems for children, two of which, in book form, have become favorites of Chandler Fischer, our three-year-old son. One, *Marsupial Sue,* is an illustrated song about a young kangaroo who decides she really likes being a kangaroo after envying other forms of mammalian existence. The other, *Micawber,* is a beautifully illustrated poem about an extraordinary squirrel with an insatiable appetite for art.

Micawber lives in a nest high atop the old carousel in New York's Central Park. Every Sunday he would scamper off to the Museum of Art on Fifth Avenue and enthrall himself with the beauty he found there. Through windows and skylights he would peer in at the likes of Rembrandt and Rubens, Titian and Rousseau. It was "a feast every week for his eyes and his heart."[2]

One particular Sunday in springtime, he became captivated by a young female art student who was copying one of
Monet's masterpieces depicting a haystack at twilight.
Micawber was riveted for hours watching her, noting every
stroke of the brush, every shade, and every texture she created. Beside himself with wonder and curiosity, he stowed
away in her paint box and bicycled home with her unawares,
where he waited until midnight to creep out of hiding, pull
out her supplies, and begin his own artistic odyssey.

It was then that Micawber's dull life began to take on creative dimensions as he discovered the wonders of color. Using
his tail as a brush, he painted all night and dizzied himself
over the beauty of his work. For the first time he discovered
the joy of creating something, not just looking at someone
else's creation. Micawber was hooked.

By the next fall, he had returned numerous times to the
home of his unwitting new friend and used her canvases and
oils to create a rather large backlog of work which he ended
up displaying on the walls of his home atop the carousel. No
longer just a nest, his home became known among the more
astute rodents, fowl, and larger insects of Central Park as
Micawber's Museum of Art. And should anyone be in the
vicinity of New York's Central Park in the summertime, they
are encouraged to look for a squirrel "with a gleam in his eye
and some paint on the tip of his tail."[3]

Art Appreciation

In this magical little book, John Lithgow has somehow
managed to capture the heart of an appreciation for art and art
history that almost equals a course in it; and he's done it, of all
things, with an imaginary squirrel. As a piece, in and of itself,
this poem is proof of the power of creativity and imagination.
So much so that I am going to ask you to stretch your own
imagination and accept little Micawber as our guide through
this final chapter, as we think about finding God in the world
of art. (I am assuming that Micawber is a Christian squirrel, or

at least a God-fearing one. For reasons I won't explore here, it's difficult to imagine a squirrel as an atheist.)

The first thing we notice is that Micawber seems to accept the beauty of what God created and what man creates with like wonder. His appreciation for the masterpieces he enjoys through the museum window is no different than his appreciation for the natural beauty of Central Park. He sees God equally in each, for he knows that God made the natural world just as he made those who captured it inside a museum. Micawber knows that the artist herself, like his unwitting teacher, is in the image of God, and merely interpreting some aspect of God's creation as she passes it along to him (and us).

What Micawber doesn't know is that he exists only in the mind of John Lithgow and those who will imagine him through this poem. This would come as a pretty big blow to his pride, so don't even think about suggesting it to him! And anyway, John Lithgow exists in the mind of God, so it's a similar thing—perhaps even a glimpse of an understanding of how God experiences us. Novelists talk about fighting and otherwise interacting personally with their characters as if they were real people. Wouldn't we expect God to have something of the same experience with us who are real? It would make Micawber feel better to know that someone thought up Mr. Lithgow as well.

At the same time, both Mr. Lithgow and Micawber have a personal autonomy that God gave them. I don't know what John Lithgow thinks of God—or if he even believes God exists—but I don't have to know the answer to that before I appreciate his work. Couldn't God create a thoughtful, talented individual to discover and create truth about his universe and yet never come to a knowledge of him or believe in him—perhaps even fight with him most of the way? And couldn't the work of that person be appreciated by those who do believe in God? Couldn't that work even be attributed to God in the believer's mind? I see no reason why not. And I see nothing but worship as a reason why.

Because Micawber is imaginary doesn't make him any less meaningful than if he were real. Through the power of story, he is real to all who have read about and imagined him. Besides, the next time I am in a park, I can guarantee that I will pay more attention to the squirrels, and especially to their tails. You never know. C.F. Payne, illustrator for the book, has captured Micawber in one of his paintings as a regular squirrel among four other squirrels, going about their business in Central Park doing what squirrels do, except that one of them—the furthest one away—has a tangerine tip on his tail. Ah, that telltale tip!

Developing Your Own Pictures

Micawber's story is all about his own experience of creativity. It is, in fact, all about the wonders of God that can be found among man-made things. I can relate to his state of being captivated in the presence of great works of art. It happened to me for the first time in my early twenties when I went traveling in Europe and spent a day in Florence, Italy, taking in its cathedrals, museums, and classical works of art such as Michelangelo's massive sculpture of David.

I ended my day on a hillside overlooking the whole city. The sky was golden, like the gold flake in the Byzantine style of sixteenth-century works I had been looking at most of the day. I wanted to capture the moment in some way, but I was out of film. Rather than be frustrated by that, I decided that maybe it was the best thing. I wondered how often I took pictures and relied on the camera to remember the moment for me, and missed a deeper experience of the thing itself. I decided to let my mind be the camera instead of the little black box. So for an hour I sat and made a mental picture of the sweep of the city. I noticed the nuances in color—colors unfamiliar to any of the places I had been so far in my life.

I noticed the shape and deep green color of the thin, tall trees that lined the roadside up to the museum parking lot where I sat. I noticed the dirtier green of the olive trees that proliferated further down the hill. I noticed the yellowing color of the houses closer to me, the laundry strung between them, and the dark green shutters that sagged on their hinges. Further away stood the city with its domes, cathedral spires, and parapets. I could even recognize some of the buildings I had visited earlier in the day. It's been over 30 years, and that picture is with me still. I'm not even sure I still have the pictures I took from that trip, but I have this one. That's because I developed it myself.

I also remember that God was a big part of what I experienced that day. It was as spiritual a day as I have ever spent. It didn't have to be. Someone else could experience the same day without acknowledging God in any way, and they would still be richly rewarded. But because I know and love God, every experience I attribute to him increases my understanding and appreciation of his ways and his wonder. Whenever I notice something beautiful, I tend to attribute it to God, whether it is art or architecture or music, and in some mystical way, I share it with him, as if he were watching with me—well, I suppose he is, actually. I do not stop to find out whether the person who created it was a Christian or whether they gave glory to God for what they did, I simply receive it as coming from my Father, who is the source of everything worthy. Beauty and truth belong to God. The Creator is still creating. We are in his presence continually. "For in him we live and move and have our being" (Acts 17:28).

Walking by faith is a way of enjoying life, not just a way of being religious. Walking and living by faith may not even appear religious at all. It may appear very human. That's only right, because as we have already discovered, God said yes to our humanity. So having fun, celebrating, dancing, and laughing are all a part of a life of faith. To be sure, sadness and grief have their season as well. But faith can accompany the whole gamut of human emotions and come out hopeful in the end. This is what tempers even our sorrow. There's a fairy-tale ending to this story.

What About Sin?

Now of course, just as in our own stories, and the story of the whole human race, at some point sin enters the picture. It might come by way of a sincere depiction of someone sinning, as we find often in the stories of the Bible, or it might come through the twisted imaginations of a perverted mind, in which case caution needs to be used. In one case, someone is trying to realistically present the human condition, which in order to be truthful will have sin somewhere in the picture; in the other, someone is trying to get me to sin along with them— justifying their own lewd thoughts by getting someone else to think them too. It's the difference between Bill Moyers and Howard Stern. There is sin as part of the human predicament, and there is sin as a commodity. One portrays sin as part of the truth, the other portrays sin in order to traffic in it. It's the difference between the story of Solomon with his numerous wives and concubines and the *Playboy* empire. To be sure, some art may toe the line between the two, but I believe an understanding of the difference can help us make more informed choices.

It should also be noted that sin is a highly personal issue. There are sins which are sins to everyone—these are made very clear in Scripture (as in the Ten Commandments)—and there are sins which are sins to some but not to others. This is where legalism raises its ugly head, drawing lines for people all over God's good creation. "Do not allow what you consider good to be spoken of as evil," says Paul (Romans 14:16 NIV). Confronting sins of conscience, Paul goes on to say, "So whatever you believe about these things keep between yourself and God. [In other words, don't make rules for others in areas that are not clearly indicated in Scripture.] Blessed is the man who does not condemn himself by what he approves. But the man who has doubts is condemned...his [actions are] not from faith; and everything that does not come from faith is sin" (Romans 14:22-23). Paul is also implying that everything

that does come from faith is to be enjoyed with a clear conscience.

An Artist's Eye

Micawber had a flair for the daring. It is what made his
life exceptional and took him beyond the dull experiences of
ordinary squirrels. It was the experience of something outside the norm that turned Micawber's life into an adventure.
I believe that God always has more for us out there, but we
stop short of it because we are unwilling to risk. If this is
God's world (and it is), we can venture out with boldness to
experience him in new ways. The museum is only one
example. Outside of those things which traffic in sin, there is
a wealth of experience of God waiting to be known and
explored. But beware: You might have to cross a few lines,
stow away in someone's paint box, or squeeze out some
colors after midnight to find it! The world, and our experience of it, will be different for each of us. We are not all artists
in the traditional sense, but we are all artists in that we were
created by one, and we are in his image.

That means there is a flair for life awaiting every believer
somewhere just beyond our reach. Something by which we
experience God's ongoing creativity. Something that will leave
some paint on our tails and a gleam in our eyes. I can't tell you
what yours is, but you might start by studying something in
the world that captures your interest, much like the museum
got ahold of Micawber. And then look for God there.

Dabbling in paint will leave its mark, but it's the gleam in
Micawber's eye I like most of all. That gleam tells me he goes
through life knowing a secret. Even though he is out with the
other squirrels, doing what squirrels do, gathering food and
preparing for winter, he still has this secret—this other thing
he does on the side, only it's become more than just something on the side. It has redefined his life and how he sees the
world around him, not to mention how it has turned his
living room into his own personal gallery.

Postscript

❖ ❖ ❖

My wife called to me the other day while she was putting on her makeup and listening to National Public Radio (NPR)—a kind of morning ritual for her.

"Hurry. They're doing a story on your college."

"No kidding?"

I was just in time to catch some country music and a square dance caller making sure everyone bowed to their partner. Then Bob Edwards, host of *Morning Edition,* came on pointing out that up until now, square dancing was the only kind of dancing allowed at Wheaton College in Illinois. But all that is about to change, as a new policy of student conduct has been approved allowing dancing on campus for the first time in the 136-year history of the flagship evangelical Christian college, with the first school-sponsored dance to be held in the fall. This announcement was celebrated on the radio show by a musical sound bite of ABBA singing "Dancing Queen."

Apparently college administrators and trustees at Wheaton have decided there is nothing in the Bible against dancing as long as it isn't "immodest, sinfully erotic, or harmfully violent." Which, of course, makes you wonder why this didn't happen a long time ago, because the Bible hasn't changed in a few thousand years. This was an admission that

181

this taboo was only a cultural thing all along. It never was biblical.

The final musical sound bite for the NPR report was taken from the song "Footloose" by Kenny Loggins, from the movie by the same name, and it finished with "...everybody cut FOOTLOOSE!" Now this song was a fitting conclusion for this unlikely news item given that film's treatment of fundamentalism and dancing. But if I were producing this story, I would have chosen something more like Carol King's "I Feel the Earth Move Under My Feet" where the stars tumbled down on top of her, because that's about how long I figured it would be before Wheaton College ever allowed dancing on its campus.

But with God, all things are possible.

As a Wheaton student in the late '60s, changing "The Pledge" (as it was called then) to allow dancing and movie-going was a minor crusade for me and many of my classmates. Indeed, this battle was pretty much the extent of "student unrest" at Wheaton in 1968. While students on university campuses across the country were rioting against civil injustice and the Viet Nam war, we were out in the streets of Wheaton protesting The Pledge.

All we wanted to do was dance.

The NPR report also mentioned that students were looking forward to learning ballroom dancing, and the ROTC students were especially excited about being able to host an annual military ball. And then there's the Washington Banquet, a yearly formal event, which up until now has been reminiscent of the typical evangelical alternative to the high school prom night—dress-up, dinner, and some entertainment. Now it can be the Washington Dinner and Dance.

Those outside of evangelical circles are undoubtedly smirking over this story—one of the main reasons, I'm sure, why it got the attention it did. People are always fascinated by these nuances in Christian conduct. Think about it. At the time of its release, America was about to go to war with Iraq. Tensions were high and the economy had fallen drastically since 9/11/01, and NPR takes the time to break the big story that you can dance at Wheaton. A week later it was a major news item in the *Los Angeles Times*.[1] It's amazing how big this stuff can get.

I can't help but think that some of this fascination is related to our judgment of secular society in general. In spite of how absurd it is to judge sinners for sinning, Christians seem to do it anyway. So whenever we loosen our grip on any kind of moral standard or cultural taboo, the world loves to gloat over our apparent inconsistency. It's a little like making the church lady do the rumba.

But maybe it isn't just that people are gloating. Maybe it really is big, and in a much bigger way than merely reversing over a century of legalistic tradition. Maybe it's time for us all to dance. Maybe of all things, Christians who have been excusing themselves from the party for so long can actually be the ones to get people up and dancing again. It's unexpected, like Jesus turning water into wine when the wine ran out and threatened to end the wedding reception. No one was expecting Jesus to care about that. Maybe now is the time to dance and not mourn—to celebrate the creation and the Creator, who called it good. And why not? Why not lead out? Oh, our steps will be funny and awkward because we don't know how to move with the music very well, but God makes the music of the universe, and he can get us up and dancing, I'm sure, without too much trouble. There is great trouble in the world, but God says to be of good cheer (which is a little like dancing) "because I have overcome the world" (John 16:33). Christians should know that.

This is big. This is even bigger than God showing up in my '57 Ford. Somebody needs to get ahold of this besides NPR. No one is expecting Christians to dance. After all, we're the ones accused of booting trick or treating, banning Harry Potter, and boycotting "the happiest place on earth."

Believe me, no one will be expecting us to be up and dancing any time soon.

But they're dancing at Wheaton. And if Wheaton College says it's okay, then kick off your shoes, baby, and everybody go footloose!

Notes

Chapter 1—Getting More of God in Your Life

1. Robert Farrar Capon, The Bell Lecture, "The Astonished Heart," October 23, 1994.

Chapter 2—It's a Material World

1. Richard Leiby, "The Pop Hymn That Everyone's Humming: 'One of Us' Came Out of the Blue and Climbed the Charts," *Washington Post*, December 19, 1995, p. B-1.
2. Ibid.
3. Brian Wren, "Good Is the Flesh," © Copyright 1989 by Hope Publishing Company, Carol Stream, IL. All rights reserved. Used by permission.
4. Ibid.
5. Source. Internet.
6. Wren, "Good Is the Flesh."

Chapter 3—Hide-and-Seek

1. Larry Wall at <http://interviews.slashdot.org/interviews/02/09/06/1343222.shtml?tid=145>.
2. Colleen McDannell, *Material Christianity: Religion and Popular Culture in America* (New Haven, CT: Yale University Press, 1996), p. 222.
3. William M. Easum and Thomas G. Brady, *Growing Spiritual Redwoods* (Nashville: Abingdon Press, 1997), p. 21.

Chapter 4—The Cultural Christian and the Christian in Culture

1. Todd Hahn and David Verhaagen, *GenXers After God: Helping a Generation Pursue Jesus* (Grand Rapid, MI: Baker Book House, 1998), p. 60.
2. David Lewellen, "Wild About Harry?" *The Repository*, (October 12, 2002), p. B-5.
3. Ibid.

Chapter 5—All Truth Is God's Truth

1. Roy Rivenburg, "Jesus in a Geo? It Would Be a Miracle" *Los Angeles Times*, (November 20, 2002), p. E-1.

2. Chris Pasles, "Speaking a Universal Language," *Los Angeles Times* (November 20, 2002), p. E-1.
3. Chap Clark, "A Theological Response to Popular Culture," in Duffy Robbins, *The Grace Adventure: An Introduction to Youth Ministry* (Grand Rapids, MI: Zondervan, forthcoming).

Chapter 6—What's Good About It?

1. David Dark, *Everyday Apocalypse* (Grand Rapids, MI: Brazos Press, 2002), p. 54.
2. Chris Seay, *The Gospel According to Tony Soprano,* <www.relevant-store.com/catalog/product_info.php?products_id=42>.

Chapter 7—Outside In

1. Eugene Peterson, *Reversed Thunder* (San Francisco: HarperSanFrancisco, 1991), p. 171.
2. Thor Ramsey. See <http://thorramsey.com/bio.htm>.

Chapter 8—Inside Out

1. Michael J. McClymond, "The Last Sexual Perversion: An Argument in Defense of Celibacy," *Theology Today* 57 (2000) pp. 217-231.
2. Ibid.
3. Dan Buck, "Getting Out of the Faith Ghetto," <www.relevant-magazine.com>, March/April, 2003, p. 44.

Chapter 11—Faith at Work

1. Press release for Jars of Clay's *The Eleventh Hour.* See <www.bpnews.net/bpnews.asp?ID=12717>.

Chapter 13—Joining the Adventure

1. Reprinted with permission of Simon & Schuster Books for Young Readers, an imprint of Simon & Schuster Children's Publishing Division from *Micawber* by John Lithgow. Text copyright © 2002 John Lithgow.
2. Ibid.
3. Ibid.

Postscript

1. Richard N. Ostling, "Wheaton College OKs Dancing but Won't Get Swept Off Its Feet," *Los Angeles Times* (March 8, 2003), p. B-17.

FEARLESS FAITH

Christian radio, Christian television, Christian schools, and Christian activism have created a cushion that protects believers from a world that often ridicules Christian beliefs and values. Is this the life of faith Christ's followers are called to? Christian leader and musician John Fischer challenges believers to break out of the safety zone and share Christ through acts of love, intelligent conversation, and genuine compassion. Readers will discover how they can...

- meet and connect with the lost

- face danger with excitement by depending on Jesus

- understand what it truly means to be "set apart"

Fearless Faith offers the encouragement and tools Christians need to step out in faith and point people to the salvation found in Jesus.

Other Books by John Fischer:

❖ ❖ ❖

Saint Ben

Ashes on the Wind

On a Hill (Too) Far Away

12 Steps for the Recovering Pharisee (like me)

Fearless Faith

❖ ❖ ❖

E-mail John at: john@fischtank.com
Or log onto his website at: www.fischtank.com

For information on booking John for a
speaking engagement contact:

John Fischer Appearances
661/325-6967

❖ ❖ ❖

DATE DUE

DEMCO 38-297